For Pete —

— with my best
wishes & kindest
regards,

John D'Arcy

July 3rd 2015.

Plate 1 The Rev. Sir Frederick A.G. Ouseley, Bt. Mus. Bac.

OUSELEY'S LEGACY

The Catholic and Gothic Revivals,
Henry Woodyer, and St Michael's College.

by

John D. Austin

With a Chapter on the Organ in Appendix One
by
Michael Hart, G.R.S.M., A.R.C.O.

© John D. Austin 2014

All rights reserved.
No unauthorised reproduction permitted.

I dedicate this book to my late, most dear, and loving wife

GILL,

who passed away on Tuesday, March 4th, 2013.

Less than a fortnight beforehand she wrote me this, a

POEM FOR VALENTINES' DAY.

It included this stanza –

And now he's down in Horsham, and writing with such power

This time the subject's Ouseley and Henry Woodyer,

For he's never lost his love of Choir School country life,

The singing of the music – you could cut it with a knife.

CONTENTS

List of Contents

Acknowledgements

List of Plates

Foreword by Christopher Robinson, C.V.O., C.B.E.

Introduction

Chapter 1	The Catholic Revival & the Oxford Movement	19
Chapter 2	The Gothic Revival	24
Chapter 3	A Brief Outline of Woodyer's Life	29
Chapter 4	The Ouseley Family Background	41
Chapter 5	Sir Frederick Ouseley's Childhood	48
Chapter 6	The Joyce Family and Dorking	70
Chapter 7	St Barnabas, Pimlico	75
Chapter 8	Love Hill House	79
Chapter 9	Building St Michael's Church and College	86
Chapter 10	From the Newspapers	112
Chapter 11	Ouseley and Elgar	120
Chapter 12	Books and Letters	126
Chapter 13	Fellowes / Colles, Pine / Symonds	142
Chapter 14	Christopher Hassall and John Betjeman	153
Chapter 15	Closure	164
Chapter 16	Service of Thanksgiving	166
Chapter 17	Personal Notes	178
Chapter 18	Sir Gore's and Sir Frederick's Libraries	183

Appendix 1	The Organ, by Michael Hart	191
Appendix 2	The Bells, by Christopher Pickford	214
Appendix 3	Biographical Details of Plate 27	219
Sources Consulted and Bibliography		224

ACKNOWLEDGEMENTS

Especially I would like to warmly thank –

Michael Hart, for the chapter on the organ but also for considerable help and guidance generally, especially on the Miller brothers.

Dr. Christopher Robinson C.V.O., C.B.E. for the Foreword.

My son-in-law Martin Cox for his great help in getting it into print.

My daughter Kate Cox for enormous help in putting it all together etc.

My grandsons Ben Cox and Sam Worskett for their help.

Valerie Pickard, for genealogical help and encouragement.

Charles Beresford for much help, especially with Plate 27.

Also –

Country Life for copyright permission on plates of Hall Barn.

Mrs Flaxman for copyright permission on the Sir Gore watercolour.

Brandwood, Dr. Geoff, former Chairman of the Victorian Society.

Judith Curthoys, Archivist, Christ Church College, Oxford.

Vivian Burgess, British Library Newspapers.

Rosalind Caird, Hereford Cathedral Library.

Rev. Dr. Alasdair Coles, Vicar of St Mary's Bourne Street and St Barnabas, Pimlico.

Joanna Cordon, The Royal Society.

Elliott, Dr John, joint editor *'Henry Woodyer, Gentleman Architect'*.

Rt. Hon. Mrs. Jennefer Farncombe.

Francesca-Jane Giles, the Grosvenor Estate.

Alan Grant, Grant and Shaw Ltd.,

Alison Kenny, City of Westminster Archives Centre.

Sheila Markham, Librarian, The Travellers Club, London.

Tony Pilmer, Local Studies Librarian, Slough Library.

and J. K. Macqueen for copyright for text and photo of Love Hill House.

Helen Porter, Royal Asiatic Society.

Rt. Hon. Lucia Whitehead of Hall Barn.

John Wilson Manuscripts, Ltd.

Diana Ingram, Librarian, Frome Museum.

And Derrik Jenkyns and John Brown for helping to make my days at St. Michael's such happy and memorable ones.

LIST OF PLATES

Plate 1 — The Rev. Sir Frederick A. G. Ouseley, Bt. Mus. Bac.

Plate 2 — The pendant vault at the church at Caudebec, where Augustin Pugin and his friends nearly got stuck.

Plate 3 — Henry Woodyer's birthplace in Guildford.

Plate 4 — Chancel arch murals by Gambier Parry at the Church of the Holy Innocents at Highnam.

Plate 5 — The banks of the River Brahmaputra, painted by Sir Gore when he was 17, and where he established a factory making Bafta fine cloth.

Plate 6 — Claramont, Sir Gore's country house.

Plate 7 — Woolmers, Sir Gore's country house.

Plate 8 — Hall Barn, Sir Gore's last home.

Plate 9 — The Rt. Hon. Sir Gore Ouseley, Bart. F. S. A. etc. Painted by R. Rothwell, R. H. A.

Plate 10 — Sir Frederick Arthur Gore Ouseley. Painted in 1837, when Ouseley was 12, by John Lucas.

Plate 11 — The Library at Hall Barn, built round a magnificent Royal Persian carpet. It was a gift from the Shah, and was brought back from the embassy.

Plate 12 — The Old Rectory, in Dorking.

Plate 13 — Dorking in 1880

Plate 14 — Love Hill House

Plate 15 — Spring Grove.

Plate 16	The Founder's grave.
Plate 17	The proposed clock and bell tower, designed by the architect C. E. Mallows in 1899. He also possibly landscaped the terraces which go down to the cricket pitch.
Plate 18	Aerial view of St. Michael and all Angels' Church and College.
Plate 19	Church interior.
Plate 20	Rev. Sir Frederick A. G. Ouseley 2nd Bt. By Lewis Carroll (Charles Lutwidge Dodgson, 1832 -1898). Date: Spring 1860.
Plate 21	St Michael's Church from the north east.
Plate 22	The Founder in 1883.
Plate 23	The author placing a wreath near the Founder's memorial in 2012, with his daughter Kate, and the Rev. Andrew Walters, the last Warden.
Plate 24	St. Michael's College and Church, November 15th, in 1862, six years after the foundation.
Plate 25	The Library as it is now, with the bust of the Founder.
Plate 26	The Library as it was originally.
Plate 27	The Tenbury Music Society Orchestra in 1866. See details in Appendix One.

FOREWORD

By

Dr. Christopher Robinson, K.C.V.O., C.B.E., Fellow.

The name of Ouseley may not be familiar to many in the wider musical world but it continues to resonate strongly, not only with those of us who attended the college which he founded, but also with many aficionados of cathedral music. How a rich baronet, priest and academic, whose childhood musical precociousness invited comparison with Mozart came to found St Michael's as a model choir school makes an inspiring story.

It is clear that cathedral music in the 19th century was in a parlous state. Any doubters should read Sir George Elvey's reminiscences of his early years at St George's Chapel Windsor. Incidentally, Elvey was the organist at the dedication service at 'St Michael's ' in 1856 and, along with his friend Ouseley and S.S. Wesley, can claim some credit for the revitalization of church music and liturgy.

My contemporaries at St Michael's in the 1940's could claim a link with the founder in the shape of Canon Alderson, that kindly clergyman from Salisbury who visited the college in his capacity as sub-warden. Alderson, in collaboration with the music critic and historian H.C. Colles compiled a history of the college which was published in 1943. It still makes excellent reading, particularly the chapter by Dr Fellowes, the librarian. Alderson's recollections of his chorister days (1878-83) are very touching, if a little idealized. Sentiment apart, there is no doubt that St Michael's always had a very distinct atmosphere, created partly by the formality of the daily services, partly by the college's location in the midst of beautiful countryside and particularly because of the grandeur and dignity of the buildings. The survival of the college over nearly 130 years speaks volumes for the strength of the founder's vision. To quote Sir Sydney Nicholson (joint acting organist 1942-44) 'There are plenty of prep schools but only one St Michael's'.

After the closure of St Michael's in 1985 two more histories appeared. Watkins Shaw's slim volume is typically scholarly. It explores more deeply the early history of the Ouseley family and gives a concise survey of the post-war years (1945-85) with particular reference to the governance of the college. Three chapters from the earlier history are reprinted and there is a close examination of the musical repertoire in Ouseley's day. David Bland's Ouseley and his angels (2000) attempts a more complete history and gives a fuller and more detailed record of the day-to-day life of the College.

John Austin's new book, which I am pleased to commend, expands further what is already known about the Ouseleys. Ecclesiastical, architectural and musical themes predominate and a vivid picture of 19th century England emerges. In my day Victorian Gothic was not widely admired but enthusiasts like Sir John Betjeman inspired a re-think and it is good to see his name among the chapter headings. Also welcome is the chapter devoted to the fine Father Willis organ, written by its custodian (and old boy) Michael Hart. He ensures that it is kept in working order and that it is played regularly.

Today St Michael's without its choir can seem a sad place. But the atmosphere of the buildings remains intact and it is a fascinating place of pilgrimage for anyone interested in church music and organs. The Ouseley Trust continues the founder's work by supporting cathedral music as generously as it can, and ensures that the name of Ouseley continues to be honoured, at any rate for the foreseeable future.

INTRODUCTION

We are going on a journey into a forgotten world, a world of moral certainties, confident prosperity, national stability, rural tranquillity and charm. To get to this world of mid-Victorian England, where the railways and the Industrial Revolution have not yet really got under way, we need to go through a portal. Portals come in all shapes and sizes. Lucy went through the back of the wardrobe and arrived in Narnia, and Alice went down the rabbit hole and arrived in Wonderland. Other portals, indeed, are the womb and the grave. The one we are going through to arrive in the world of The Oxford Movement, The Cambridge Camden Society and The Gothic Revival, is the 1856 foundation of the Church of St Michael and All Angels and St Michael's College, with its Pugin inspired pointed arches, outside Tenbury Wells.

It has been well said that St Michael's College was the creation of two men, the patron, the Rev. Sir Frederick Ouseley, Bt. who gave it life and spirit, and his architect, Henry Woodyer, who gave it body. When we think about the place, and I went there as a boy when I was nine years old, we feel Ouseley's enduring influence on our lives in various ways, but when we picture the place in our minds eye it is Woodyer's buildings that we see. It is not possible to think about the one without seeing the other. The two men had one great principle in common, of dedicating their personal life and purpose to the greater glory of God. Ouseley achieved this by his devotion to the improvement of choral aspects of the music of the church. Woodyer only took on architectural work which he believed matched up to his principles.

This book is in the nature of a miscellany. The history of the College has already been detailed to a greater or lesser extent in five books. These are *'Memorials of Frederick Arthur Gore Ouseley, Bart'* by Rev. Francis T. Havergal, *'The Life of Sir F.A.G. Ouseley, Bart'* by F. W. Joyce, *'The History of St Michael's College, Tenbury'*, by M. F. Alderson and H. C. Colles, *'Sir Frederick Ouseley and St Michael's Tenbury'*, Ed. by Watkins Shaw, and lastly *'Ouseley and his Angels'* by David Bland. These will be referred to in the text as *'Havergal'*, *'Joyce'*, *'Alderson/Colles'*, *'Watkins Shaw'* and *'Bland'*.

A miscellany seemed to be an appropriate description of what follows, as the successive chapters cover a variety of subjects, with wide-ranging aspects of the central theme. It is very surprising how little Henry Woodyer is mentioned in the five books on St Michael's, apart from in Charles Nicholson's article in *'Alderson/Colles'*.

The chapter on Henry Woodyer is a fairly comprehensive article about Woodyer's family, his days at Eton with his life-long friend Thomas Gambier Parry, whose son was Hubert Parry, the composer, and of his Oxford years. Writing about Woodyer's architectural training and the architectural and ecclesiastical world of his formative years is essential in trying to understand the building that he designed for Ouseley. These pages are followed by sections on Ouseley's childhood and his early years before he met Woodyer. I have done research especially on Hall Barn, near Beaconsfield, which Sir Gore bought in 1832 and where Frederick lived from aged seven to fifteen. Particularly interesting are the photographs of the huge south wing that Sir Gore added on to the mansion for the visit of King William IV and Queen Adelaide, and which was demolished in 1969. These include the fine library which he had built to the dimensions of the magnificent Royal Persian carpet given to him by the Shah. Here he housed his valuable collection of six or seven thousand volumes for which Sir Frederick subsequently built the library at St Michael's. Living in such surroundings obviously inspired Frederick to collect his own library, which he devoted entirely to music. Hall Barn is now privately owned and is not open to the public.

Michael Hart has very kindly accepted my request to write a chapter on the organ at St Michael's Church. He deals in detail with the problems of the water damaged Flight organ, with its extraordinary Tuba Mirabilis Pipes *en chamade*. These were mounted horizontally, in front of the organ case, projecting out over the choir stalls. They produced a commanding, loud trumpet-like tone, which was used for fanfares and solos. Sir Frederick was bitterly disappointed that this instrument was not in full working order for the consecration of the church.

Michael Hart goes on to record in detail the row between Sir Frederick and Harrisons, the next organ builder he tried, and then the final solution in 1873 of the Father Willis organ, which is still in the church today – a hundred and forty years later, and still sounding just as splendidly powerful. It took Sir Frederick seventeen years before he had an instrument that satisfied him.

When Mozart called the pipe organ *The King of Instruments* in 1776 he was speaking from fourteen year's experience. He began playing the instrument when he was seven, and was quite unable to reach the pedals. This would have been not unlike like Christopher Robinson, whom I saw playing the piano, which had pedals, in the Dining Hall gallery when he was about twelve.

Dr. Christopher Robinson, K.C.V.O. has very kindly accepted my request to write the Foreword.

It is my hope that this book will be of interest to a wider field of people other than those immediately connected with St Michael's Church and the College. There is a growing appreciation and understanding of the Victorian entrepreneurs, artists, engineers and architects, especially Pugin and his followers. In this book I have tried to set out the relationships between patron and architect and other people involved such as stained glass suppliers. It may be only about one church and its associated college building but it is representative of much else in the national landscape of Gothic revival architecture of that era, and the influence of the Oxford Movement and the Catholic Revival.

It is worth emphasising that Ouseley defined his life's work in the College Statutes of 1864 -

'Whereas Sir Frederick Arthur Gore Ouseley Bt. resolved to establish a college for the religious, musical and secular education and training of boys, with an especial view to this becoming qualified to promote the devout and effective celebration of the Choral Services of the Established Church of England and Ireland, for the purposes of promoting such devout and effective celebration by exhibiting a model for the same'.

Indeed, this is what St. Michael's is all about.

If you take the initial letter of the first word of the first five Chapters, which are A – M – G – P – D, you will find they are the same as the initial letter of the first five words of the 'Hail Mary', in Latin, of course. Had I been alive in the Reformation days of Queen Elizabeth I, this covert message would have resulted in me being burned at the stake.

John D. Austin.

CHAPTER ONE

THE CATHOLIC REVIVAL

AND THE OXFORD MOVEMENT

Any writing about High Church Anglicanism must start with the Oxford Movement. The stage must be set for all that followed, which includes Ouseley's inspired mind-set. Much has been written about the history of the English Church, but no event since St. Augustine landed in A.D. 597, is so pivotal as the story of the Oxford Movement. This was a movement of High Church Anglicans, which eventually developed into Anglo-Catholicism. The precise moment when this innovation began was July 14th 1833, when a sermon was preached before His Majesty's Judges of Assize at Oxford by Mr John Keble, the most distinguished of the distinguished Fellows of Oriel College, at St Mary the Virgin, the University Church. The subject of the sermon was National Apostacy. It has been said that the sermon was '*a ringing call to Churchman to realise the immediate danger in which the Church of England stood, and rally to her aid*'. In Hanoverian times the Church had become apathetic and stagnant; convocations were ineffective, daily services ignored, holy days unobserved and pastoral work neglected. More particularly they felt that the church had become controlled more by Parliament than by the Bishops, i.e. Eurasian, and had become secular. The churches throughout the land were in a deplorable state. In many places Baptisms were totally neglected and the fonts filled with rubbish. A Communion Service was held perhaps once a year. The Bishop of London recorded that in 1800 there were only six communicants in St. Paul's Cathedral on Easter Day. The altar was a rickety table that served more as a convenient place for the minister's overcoat, hat, and riding crop. There was no cross. In the centre aisle there was the three-decker pulpit – an enormous piece of furniture. At the bottom stood the clerk who read the Parish Notices, in the centre stood the verger who read all the psalms, and he alone read them, and at the top was the cleric who preached, and the sermons were long, and I mean long; two hours were not unusual. Plurality and non-residence were rife, where Ministers had the advantages of the tithes of many parishes and hardly ever visited any of their churches, and where Bishops were worldly and wealthy and often did not even live in their diocese. In short, the words of Thomas Arnold, written in 1832, must have seemed to be thinking persons of his day to summarise the entire situation: *"No human power can save the Church as it now stands."*

In the same year John Henry Newman, who was vicar of the University Church of St Mary the Virgin, fully supported Keble, putting the arguments in the first of the 'Tracts for the Times'. Over the following eight years ninety 'Tracts for the Times' were written and the group became known as Tractarians. It was as if they felt that the Reformation had gone too far, and that a split from the domination of the Roman Catholic Church could have been achieved without abandoning the importance of the Eucharist, observance of holy days, certain rituals and so forth. It was as if that at the Reformation, and the simile is perhaps slightly unfortunate, the baby had been thrown out with the bathwater.

The Oxford Movement gained its name from a small, enthusiastic and scholarly group of young Oxford Fellows, all at Oriel College, who bravely launched the great adventure that was to reawaken the Anglican Church to the glories of its ancient catholic heritage. Informally grouped around the slightly older John Keble, they became increasingly outspoken about the needs and shortcomings of the contemporary church. These were heady times in England. Catholic Emancipation had come in 1829, and the forces around the Reform Act of 1832 were felt in all walks of life. The old status quo was being threatened, but many questions about church government and doctrines left unanswered. There was a feeling that there was everything to play for. In Dean Church's word, the leading figures of the Oxford Movement were *'men of large designs'*. They were in fact vastly different men in character including: John Keble, shy and retiring… Hurrell Froude, playful, venturesome… John Henry Newman, sensitive and scholarly…Isaac Williams, a first-rate Harrow cricketer and

Latinist, and like Keble, one of the future poets of the movement, and Edward Pusey, one of the most distinguished scholars of his day who gave a strong and certain leadership.

What these men wanted was nothing new. What they set out to revive was firmly bedded in the Bible and the Prayer Book, but had grown dusty and mouldy with neglect. All of them may be summed up in the conception of the Church as a Divine Society, repositioning the Eucharist as the central act of worship, and reintroducing the use of vestments, ceremonial, acts of piety, the sacraments, the Real Presence, Transubstantiation, Confession, the religious life, devotion to the Blessed Virgin Mary and so forth as vital personal channels of grace. For the record this is precisely where I stand. These had long been prohibited in the English church.

A natural channel for the Movement's energies lay in those fine arts which more directly serve the worship of God – architecture, painting and music, but we are interested here only with the architecture. Much work was done by members of the Movement to introduce a more medieval style of church furnishing in many churches. This was done by the formation of The Cambridge Camden Society, which became the Ecclesiological Society, of which I am a member. Neo-Gothic in many different forms became the norm rather than the earlier Neo-Classical forms. Although the Gothic Revival was foreshadowed by Horace Walpole's **Strawberry Hill** and William Beckfords's **Fonthill Abbey**, it sprung in part from the same source as the Oxford Movement, i.e. the Caroline Divines of the seventeenth century. Its greatest exponent was Augustus Welby Pugin; a fascinating man of enormous energy and religious zeal. He converted to the Roman Church. In his short lifetime of barely forty years he designed 28 country houses, 20 institutions – abbeys, convents etc, and over 45 churches.

Sometimes the opposition to the Oxford Movement erupted in violence. The vicar of St Barnabas, Rev W. J. E. Bennett was a passionate member of the Oxford Movement and in 1850 he had started introducing Tractarian ritual into his church, resulting in the 'No Popery Riots' on November 10th. The rioting crowds were dangerous and Mr. Bennett and his curate, who happened to be the twenty-seven year old Sir Frederick Ouseley, were threatened in the streets, forcing them both eventually to resign. Ouseley had been at Christ Church, Oxford, in 1843 when Newman resigned as vicar of St Mary's and in 1845 when he converted to the Roman Church.

It cannot be over-emphasised what an enormous debt of gratitude the Church of England today owes to that handful of Oriel College Fellows.

THE ANGLO-CATHOLIC HISTORY SOCIETY

The Society was formed in 2000 and seeks to promote the study of the history of the Anglo-Catholic movement in the Anglican Communion. This includes the High Church movements from the late sixteenth century as well as the Oxford Movement itself, Ritualism and Anglo-Catholicism in the nineteenth and twentieth centuries, both in England and elsewhere. The Society meets three times a year in various London churches for a lecture – these are usually held in early October, late January and June.

THE ECCLESIALOGICAL SOCIETY.

The Cambridge Camden Society, later known as the Ecclesiological Society was a learned architectural society founded in 1839 by undergraduates at Cambridge University to promote "the study of Gothic Architecture, and of Ecclesiastical Antiques. Its activities would come to include publishing a monthly journal, *The Ecclesiologist*, advising church builders on their blueprints, and advocating a return to a medieval style of church architecture in England. At its peak influence in the 1840s, the Society counted over 700 members in its ranks, including bishops of the Church of England, deans at Cambridge University, and Members of Parliament. The Society and its publications enjoyed wide influence over the design of English churches throughout the 19th century.

The Society is still very active today and includes in its membership, architects, ministers of the church, historians, church goers and just everyone who is interested in churches. I have been a member for some years.

CHAPTER TWO

THE GOTHIC REVIVAL

The Pointed Arch

Most scholars agree that pointed arch originated in the Muslim world. Probably the earliest known example is the Al-Aqsa Mosque which was built on the Temple Mount in Jerusalem c. 750 A.D. The invention of the pointed arch made it possible to make a fundamental change in the design of buildings. The weight of an upper wall which is supported by a semi-circular or round arch exerts a sideways thrust requiring massive lower walls and buttresses. When the weight is supported by a pointed arch the thrust changes from a lateral to a vertical thrust. This enabled builders to lighten the walls, build to greater heights and to bridge over different widths at any required height. A round arch could only be half as high as it is wide, but the pointed arch could vary greatly in its proportions, pointing ever upwards in increasingly tall buildings. Additionally, the use of the pointed arch also allowed vaulting for any ground plan, rather than just a square ground plan as before. Heavy buttresses were replaced by light flying buttresses. These few sentences describe a Gothic cathedral with very tall naves and chancels, staggeringly intricate vaulted roofs and flying buttresses, and it is all achieved by using the pointed arch instead of the round arch.

However, let us return to the origin of what the French call *'arc brisé'*. This means 'broken arch', which comes from the fact that it is made from two arch segments, i.e. two broken pieces of an Norman arch.

Abbot Suger (1081-1151), of the Abbey Church of St Denis, was a visionary who saw much of the world in terms of light. People were *'smaller lights'*, Christ was the *'first radiance'* and God was *'Father of*

Lights'. Suger saw the Gothic cathedral as a gateway to spiritual enlightenment.

The religious upheavals caused by the Oxford Movement can be seen in the enormous upsurge of new churches and church schools which were built on Tractarian principles, often in new suburbs and towns from the 1840's to the 1870's. At this time English architecture was also beginning a new phase of professionalism. Apart from great men like Wren, architects in the past had been regarded either as builders or semi-amateurs who left the details of their designs to masons and plasterers. The most influential of these Tractarian architects was undoubtedly Augustus Welby Northmore Pugin who was born in 1812, and died from insanity brought on by pressure of work before he reached the age of forty. It is generally recognised that Pugin started the Victorian Gothic Revival. From an early age he felt that it was only the pointed arch which pointed to heaven, that the Classical style of Wren and others was pagan, and that Gothic was the only true Christian style. It is easy to see where this started.

Auguste Charles Pugin, A.W.N. Pugin's father, was a draughtsman and ran a drawing school in London. He was born in France in 1762, and just managed to get across to England before the French Revolution. Young Augustus was born in 1812 and attended some of his father's drawing classes from an early age. In the autumn of 1824 the family crossed to France in preparation for a book on medieval architectural of Normandy, a subject of increasing interest in Britain. The party travelled in one of the large French stagecoaches of the time, the Pugins inside and the pupils on top. They did a round trip of 100 miles, visiting Caen, Rouen, and Bayeux, drawing the buildings as they went. (This would make a good film!). In Caudebec-en-Cau they went to the Eglise Notre Dame, where, in the Lady Chapel, there is a very large pendant keystone. In a current guide book on the church it says *'If you look up, there is a huge pendant suspended from the vaulted stone ceiling. It is unbelievable, and is truly set off by the glowing stained glass window. This huge (seven feet) pendant is actually a keystone and there is a little plaque explaining how the stones are set. Amazing . . .'* In order to see how the pendant vault was constructed, Pugin Senior had a hole made above it and lowered some of the smaller boys inside to draw what they saw. At that time it was perfectly easy, if hazardous, to interfere with medieval buildings in this way. When they had finished their drawings, the boys had considerable difficulty getting out again. One of them was Benjamin Ferrey, who was aged thirteen, and later became a well-known architect with about fifty parish churches and the rather splendid Royal Bath Hotel in Bournemouth to his credit. He said afterwards that he had panicked because he was larger than the others and he thought he was going to get stuck. It was in this way that Pugin learned the basic principles of a Gothic building.

When they returned to London, and all the drawings were finished the Pugins, father and son, published *'Specimens of the Antiquities of Normandy'* in 1827. There is a illustration of this extraordinary pendant vault in Pugin's book of 1827. (See Plate 2).

This work remained in print, in various editions, for over a hundred years becoming the standard reference for Gothic architecture, and a cornerstone in the Gothic Revival movement. I have a copy with Sir Gore's bookplate in it. This is very interesting because the young Frederick may well have browsed through this book in his father's library at Hall Barn before he went up to Oxford, and indeed may have been inspired by the illustrations of the gothic architecture as the style he chose for St Michael's church and college.

The origin of the Islamic pointed arch and its introduction into Europe after the First Crusade and the Fall of Jerusalem in 1099, is detailed in Chapter Two. Interestingly, it was the seventeenth century antiquary Sir William Dugdale who made the deepest and most lasting impression on Pugin. Dugdale's *Monasticon Anglicanum*, published 1655 – 73, is a great lament for the lost treasures of the monasteries. It portrays pre-Reformation England as a landscape of Gothic churches and abbeys, a world of social harmony and piety, brutally and illegally violated by Henry VIII. Dugdale was far from a neutral historian. He fought at the battle of Edgehill and when Charles I moved his Court to Oxford, Dugdale did research for his *Monasticon* at the Bodleian Library.

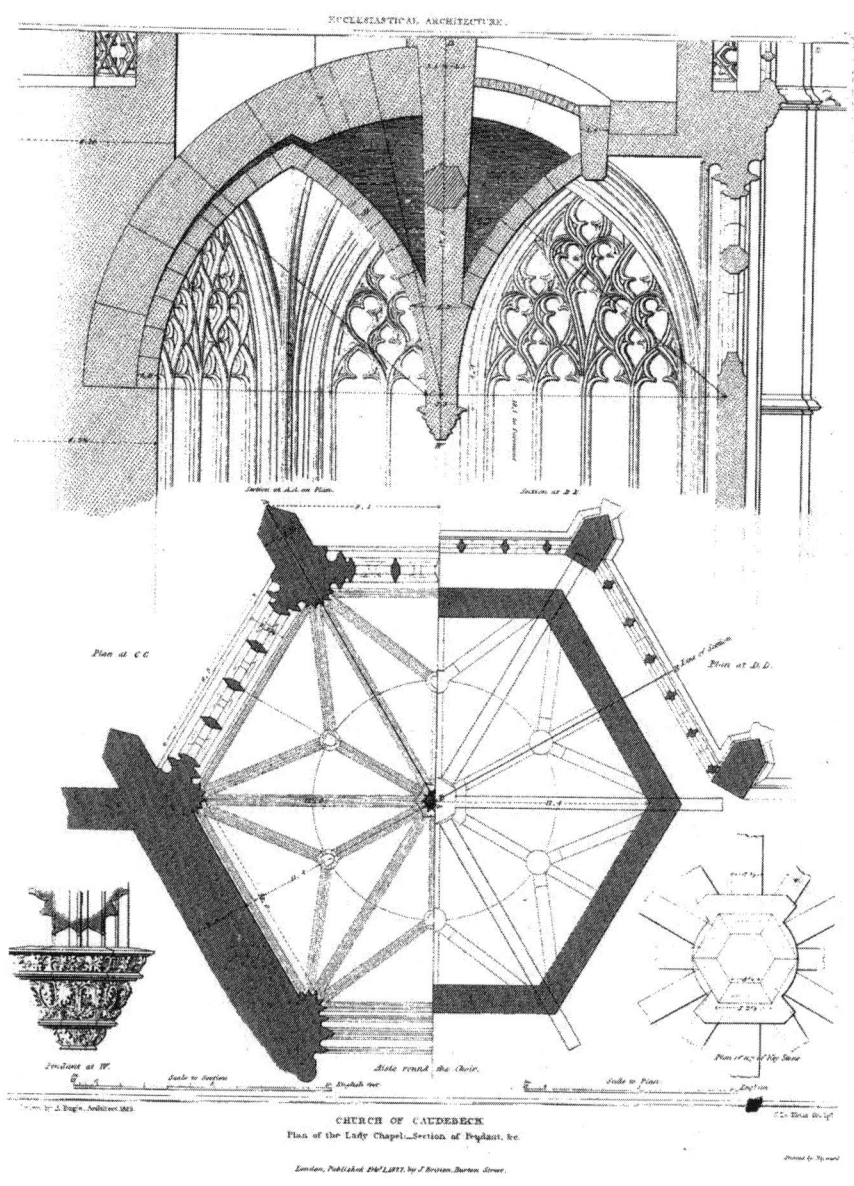

Plate 2 The pendant vault at the church at Caudebec, where Augustin Pugin and his friends nearly got stuck.

A Royalist and a High Church man, he took the view that the English Church, despite Henry's interventions, remained Catholic, but independent from Rome, continuing after the Reformation by direct apostolic descent. This was precisely, of course, Keble and Newman's argument nearly two hundred years later. Pugin's energy was staggering. By the time he was thirty he had designed twenty-two churches, three cathedrals, half a dozen houses and a Cistercian monastery. For eight years he worked with Charles Barry on the Palace of Westminster creating its great interiors, the House of Lords and the 'Big Ben' clock tower. As mentioned above Pugin died insane and disillusioned through overwork, but he had changed not only the look but also the thinking of British architecture. Pugin's doctor said that he had crammed one hundred year's work into his forty years.

It is generally recognised that Pugin started the Victorian Gothic Revival. From an early age he felt that it was only the pointed arch which pointed to heaven, that the Classical style of Wren and others was pagan, and that Gothic was the only true Christian style.

CHAPTER THREE

A BRIEF OUTLINE OF WOODYER'S LIFE

Good architecture abounded in Victorian England, but the work of Henry Woodyer made a distinctive mark. He was born in the same decade as Scott, Pugin, Pearson and Butterfield. Pugin led them all into the serious early Victorian phase of the Gothic Revival when the Middle Pointed or Geometric Style was the ultimate ideal in church design. Woodyer based his practice on churches, and in many of these he aspired to this ideal.

Woodyer was a prolific architect with over 300 commissions to his credit, but first and foremost he was a romantic gentleman with a deeply religious faith. Whilst at Oxford he became involved with the Anglican High Church Movement; and throughout his career he saw his work as an architect as a means of serving the church. His work is predominantly muscular Gothic, in the spirit of A.W.N. Pugin, from whom he may have had some early training. His was a convincing vision of the Middle Ages which he neatly encapsulated in buildings like The Church of St Michael's and All Angels and the College.

He was born on April 16th 1816 in Allen House (See Plate 3) in Guildford, the third child and only son of Caleb Woodyer (1766-1849) and his wife Mary, nee Halsey. His mother came from a wealthy family who owned Henley Park, just outside Guildford. Caleb Woodyer was not only a successful and highly regarded surgeon and male midwife, but also an astute businessman. He had bought Allen House, a large family home close to Holy Trinity Church in March 1816, for £3,000, and later he bought the house next door and other property in The Shambles in Guildford.

Plate 3 Henry Woodyer's birthplace in Guildford, Surrey.

Allen House stood opposite the Royal Grammar School from the late seventeenth century until 1964 when it was demolished. It was a large house set in extensive grounds that took its name from Anthony Allen, Master of Chancery and Mayor of Guildford in 1740. The building had many associations with the School. It was used as a boarding house from 1866 to 1874. In 1914, the grounds were purchased by H.A. Powell, and given to the school as playing fields. From 1918, Allen House was rented for use by the Grammar School and in 1921 it was purchased by Surrey County Council. It continued to be used by the RGS until its demolition in 1964.

Caleb Woodyer could afford to give his son a good education and he decided, possibly at the suggestion of Dr. Robert Keate who later became the President of the Royal College of Surgeons, to send Henry to Eton, where Robert Keate's brother John was Headmaster. The school's rather splendid full title is The King's College of Our Lady of Eton besides Wyndsor. Woodyer went to Eton in April, 1829. His tutor was Mr. Oakes, and he boarded with a Miss Bearblock. Woodyer and came under the influence of Edward Coleridge, who was his Housemaster. Coleridge was a nephew of the poet Samuel Taylor Coleridge and was to become an active follower of the Oxford Movement, or Tractarians as they were known (see below). Edward Coleridge was passed over for the post of headmaster in 1853. Although it was generally recognized that he had the best qualifications for the post, it became widely known that he was rejected on account of his strong 'High Church' sympathies. At the time this was attributed to the more Protestant Fellows of the College but it later transpired that his real opponents were the Queen and Prince Albert.

Whilst at Eton Woodyer also came into contact with William Evans who taught drawing. Evans was a talented landscape and portrait artist who painted exclusively in watercolours. In 1828 he became an associate of the Old Watercolour Society, and a friend of Ruskin and Pugin. Edward Coleridge was both a pupil and collector of Evans' works. More importantly to us Evans taught drawing to Thomas Gambier Parry (1816-1888), who became a lifelong friend of Woodyer's. Evans was also interested in architecture and some of his pupils became involved in the rediscovery of medieval decoration. Was this a foreshadowing hint of the Gothic Revival? There is no evidence to suggest that Woodyer had drawing lessons from Evans – however, comments from one of his staff about the fact that Woodyer was no draughtsman indicate that perhaps he could have done with some. Whilst at Eton Woodyer became known as a good sportsman, playing football and rowing in a College Eight for three consecutive years from 1831. In addition, in his last year he rowed in the Upper Sixes and, on 19 July 1838, took part in a race between the Six and the Eight. Gambier Parry went to Eton in January 1830, a year later than Woodyer, and left probably at Easter 1832 . Some years after he had left his brother-in-law, the Rev. William Lawrence Eliot, became an Assistant Master at Eton.

Woodyer left Eton probably at Easter 1834 and he went up to Merton College, Oxford, in 1835. The University at this time was a hot-bed of religious fervour, as seen above, and it is very probable that this had a strong influence on him; certainly he was a devout 'High Church' man throughout his later life. Not much is known about his time at Oxford. However, when he first went to Merton, he lived in a garret over 'Oxon Quare' on Lamp Staircase in the Front Quad, paying 10s. a quarter, but after that he lived in the Junior Chaplain's Rooms for the rest of his time at the college paying £1-50s. a quarter. Gambier Parry says Woodyer was 'a boating man' and there is evidence of this in a boat club account book for 1838-9 is signed and presumably written by him as Captain of Boats and Stroke.

What happened to Woodyer between 1838, when he graduated from Merton with a B.A. degree, and 1845 when he built his first church at Wyke, in Surrey, is not at all clear. He was certainly at home on June 6th 1841 because his name can be seen on the Census Return. He felt that he needed a profession that would satisfy his religious convictions, but taking Holy Orders was not his line. He also wanted to satisfy his artistic skills and interests, and at the same time maintain his life as a gentleman. He dropped on the idea of being an architect; but it is not at all clear as to where he trained although a connection with Pugin or Butterfield does seem a possibility. He began to practice independently in 1846, working mainly in Surrey and Berkshire, operating from 108 High Street, Guildford, the same address as his father's surgery. In 1845-6 he built his first complete church. He was commissioned by his brother-in-law, Lannoy Arthur Coussmaker, of Westwood, to design St Mark's Church at Wyke. His father, Caleb, died in 1849, and was buried at Wyke, leaving him properties in Stoke-juxta-Guildford and Guildford, including an asylum. This new wealth, added to income from his steadily growing architectural practice, meant that Woodyer was now financially secure.

St. Mark's was a simple early middle-pointed structure of coursed Bargate stone consisting of a 23ft chancel, 49ft nave, south-western porch and western bell-cote. The quoins were of Heath stone, the window surrounds Bath stone, the chancel was paved with Chichester tiles, and the windows glazed with Powell's quarries, except the east window which contained stained glass. The church was consecrated on 24 November 1846 but little used until late in 1847 when a new parish was formed. In 1845 the *Ecclesiologist* reported that the church would *'confer the greatest credit on the architect'*, writing that *'we have not often seen a village church superior to this'*.

Woodyer's connection with Pugin is tenuous, and it is impossible to prove that he had architectural training from him, but there were connections. Woodyer's brother-in-law's father was the Rev. Lawrence William Eliot, vicar of Peper Harrow, a parish five miles from Guildford. Lord Middleton, who owned the estate, employed Pugin from 1841 to 1848 to restore the church of St Nicholas, extensive renovations to Mousehill House, a cowfold, a barn, two gatehouses, and a bridge. Woodyer's name appears in Pugin's diary for 1845 and he may well have been employed as the clerk of works. This sounds reasonable enough but not only is Pugin well known for not having pupils, but in his writing he strongly criticized the pupillage system. He would just recommend that a trainee architect should go out and study medieval buildings. Presumably the peak of his ideals would have been late 12th C. to mid-13th C. French Gothic buildings such as Chartres Cathedral and the Sainte Chapelle.

It has been alternatively suggested that Woodyer was perhaps a pupil of William Butterfield, who was born in 1814 and died in 1900. Butterfield was an important and High Victorian Gothic architect. His father had a chemist's shop in the Strand and William was apprenticed to a builder who went bankrupt before his apprenticeship had finished. Although his family were strict non-conformists he drew religious inspiration from the Oxford Movement, starting architectural studies under E. L. Blackburne in 1833, the year of John Keble's iconic sermon. He established his own business in London in 1840, and built up a large architectural practice. In 1844 he became a member of the Ecclesiological Society and from then on, most of his work was in restoring or building churches, one of the best known and most beautiful of which is the interior of All Saints, Margaret Street, in London. He was well known for his Pugin-esque correctness in recalling Gothic forms. John Keble died in 1866 and Keble College which was founded in his memory was the *'final triumph of the Oxford Movement'*, according to Pevsner. It must have given Butterfield an enormous satisfaction to be chosen by the Founders as the architect of the new college which was started in 1868 and finished in 1882. The architecture of the College can be called a summing up of Butterfield's ideals as well as his motifs. The red brick buildings with polychrome patterns may not be to everyone's liking but Butterfield said that he *'had a mission to give dignity to brick'*. Butterfield's work at Rugby School including the exciting Chapel, built 1868-72, was Keble College but on a smaller scale.

It would seem that Woodyer had a stronger connection with Butterfield as far as training or apprenticeship is concerned than he might have had with Pugin. Gambier Parry said that after Woodyer had decided to become an architect he put himself into an architect's office. The architect Harry Redfern wrote an article in 1944, when he was 83 years old, called *'Some Recollections of William Butterworth and Henry Woodyer'*. Remembering what he had heard as a boy in Woodyer's office in the 1870s, he wrote *'During the long course of his practice Butterfield had only two pupils. The first and by far the most important was Henry Woodyer, not many years his junior (there was only two years between them). He entered the office sometime after coming down from Oxford'*. In addition to this, Woodyer's name as an architect is in the London Post Office directories from 1846 to 1857. His address is given as 4, Adam Street, the address in Adelphi which is where Butterfield lived and worked. This is all very positive, but the two men did have very opposite backgrounds and temperaments. Woodyer was a gentleman, Eton and Oxford and a romantic, whilst Butterfield was decidedly trade, quiet and introspective. What was much more important was that in terms of building techniques and architectural knowledge Butterfield would have had a great deal to offer, and of course the two men were on a High Church high, living and working to the Greater Glory of God.

In 1849 Woodyer was commissioned to restore the church of St Blaise at Milton, near Abingdon, where J. S. Bowles, a contemporary at Oxford, was churchwarden . It was through this connection that he was introduced to Bowles' sister, Frances Martha, who was then eighteen years old, but they waited until she was twenty-one before they got married. The wedding took place on 5th August 1851 at Milton, the service was conducted by the Rev. Thomas Bowles, Frances' brother. The newly married couple went to live with Woodyer's mother at Allen House. Frances Martha had a daughter on June 2nd 1852, and the baby was christened Hester Fanny in Holy Trinity Church, Guildford, on 8th June. Tragically, her mother Frances Martha died nineteen days later on June 21st. Frances was buried in the crypt under the chancel of the church in Milton. Hester Fanny had been left £1,000 by her mother.

Woodyer subsequently bought a small estate at Grafham from James Steadman, a partner in his father's practice. This was an attempt, encouraged by his growing wealth, to pick up the threads of his life.

TWO OTHER WOODYER CHURCHES

The Church of the Holy Innocents, Highnam.
The Church of St Andrews, Grafham.

In order to further understand the work of Woodyer, it seemed a good idea to include one of his other churches. His lifelong friend, Gambier Parry, commissioned him to build Holy Innocents' at Highnam as a memorial to his wife, and Woodyer built St Andrews at Grafham as a memorial to his own wife. This reflected its purpose in serving as a memorial not only to his wife but also to their children who had died in infancy.

The Church of the Holy Innocents at Highnam, two miles west of Gloucester is widely regarded as Woodyer's finest church and an important monument to the Oxford Movement. It is certainly the focal point of a fine group of parochial buildings which he designed consisting of church, parsonage, school and sexton's lodge. It was Woodyer's first major work and according to Pevsner, the church is 'an immensely impressive building'. The architect Harry Goodhart-Rendel, who trained in the offices of Sir Charles Nicholson, said it was 'the fulfilment of the Pugin ideal'. The Highnam Estate, which included Highnam Court, was acquired by Thomas Gambier Parry, Woodyer's close friend of their Eton and Oxford days, in 1837 when he was twenty one. Both of Parry's parents had died when he was young and he was brought up by aunts. However his father and grandfather had been directors of the East India Company and he inherited considerable wealth. He was a connoisseur, a notable collector of medieval and renaissance art and an artist of some talent, as will be seen. He had the same Tractarian religious ideals as Woodyer; he was an early member of the Cambridge Camden Society and also a prominent member of the Ecclesiological Society. Two years after buying the Highnam Estate, he married Isabella Fynes-Clinton and together they planned to build a church for the use of the local community, but fate intervened. Only two of their six children survived to adulthood and Isabella died only twelve days after the birth of Charles Hubert Hastings Parry, the composer. The death of his wife galvanised Gambier Parry into action and he commissioned Woodyer to build The Church of the Holy Innocents. The unusual dedication, which refers to the infants that Herod ordered to be killed, can be seen also to apply to his wife, and to his children who had died in infancy, and to whom the church was built as a memorial.

The foundation stone of Holy Innocents' was laid in July 1849. It is a large and spectacular church for a country estate, with a very tall clerestoried nave with north and south aisles and high five-bay arcades. The emphasis is on verticality, expressed through the steeply pitched roofs and the relative narrowness of the proportions, especially the dormer windows in the nave roof. The story of the design of the spire is interesting. Originally, Woodyer planned a tower with crenulations with four pinnacles. However in May 1850, ten months after the foundation stone of the church was laid, and the building of the tower was up to the belfry windows, it seems Gambier Parry changed his mind. In one of his notebooks Parry wrote *'at about this time Woodyer and I were conversing about the way in which we could improve the turrets at the corner of the tower, the design was lying on the carpenters' bench in the temporary workshop on the south side of the church. I took a clumsy pencil and sketched a spire at a careless venture, without the least intending to realise it. It became however that it was the right and only thing to do'*. Woodyer was charmed with the opportunity of exercising his skill and taste and not long after this he completed his design for it. Myers estimated it at about £1,700. This was *'exceedingly cheap for such work for it is as lofty as that at Cheadle'*. Parry's reference to Pugin's Roman Catholic masterpiece at Cheadle is very interesting as Highnam is undoubtedly its Anglo-Catholic rival or equal. St Giles at Cheadle had been finished only three years earlier. In the event, a fine 200ft spire was built, which complements the whole design splendidly. What is also fascinating about this is the story that Ouseley, in 1856, also budgeted for a tower for St Michael's, but his money did not stretch that far. A drawing of this tower has so far not been found. One can perhaps assume it would have been very similar to the tower at Holy Innocents. What has been found however, in the "Academy Architecture and Architectural Review" of 1899, is a 'Clock Tower and Campanile designed for St Michael's College, Tenbury, by C.E. Mallows' (see Plate 17). All the original furnishings at Holy Innocents are preserved: canopied and crocketed reredos, octagonal stone font with a tall spire-like cover and fine iron screens. Much of this is obviously echoed in the architecture of Sᵗ Michael's which was built just five years later. The decoration of the interior is simply quite extraordinary. Gambier Parry was an artist of some distinction and over a number of years he covered nearly all the walls with paintings of figurative scenes and decorative patterning. He made a study of the technique used by Italian painters of the 14th and 15th centuries and invented 'spirit fresco', a dry plaster method suitable for the damp English climate, using a mixture of resins, oil and wax. The total effect of Gambier Parry's painting is stunning. (See Plate 4) He was quite justified in his 'spirit fresco' technique and although the paintings have largely withstood the passage of time, they have recently been restored. It is this riot of internal colour in contrast to the monochrome of Woodyer's exterior which is the glory of Highnam.

It is worth comparing this church, particularly the wall paintings and decorations, with Pugin's Sᵗ Giles at Cheadle in Staffordshire. Before leaving Holy Innocents' with its story of being built as a memorial to Gambier Parry's wife and their infant children, it is worth recalling the similarity with Woodyer's life. Henry's father Caleb Woodyer died in 1849 and left his son a considerable fortune including several properties in Guildford. This meant that Henry was now financially secure and, like Gambier Parry, he bought himself a country estate. Woodyer first met his future wife Frances Martha Bowles when she was eighteen years old and when she was twenty-one they married. The following summer Frances died a few days after giving birth to their daughter Hester. In 1860 Woodyer built Sᵗ Andrew's Church, which is near his home at Grafham in Surrey, as a memorial to his wife. Apart from their Eton and Oxford days, the two men did indeed have much in common. The plan and general arrangement of Sᵗ Andrew's follow Woodyer's rural church model, with a nave, chancel and a western bell-cote. However here the chancel is apsidal, the simple Early English lancets stand out, piercing the eaves, the bell-cote is more like a mini spire and the western doorway is a stunning mixture of mouldings. The alabaster font was made in 1854 and stood in the front hall of Grafham House, Woodyer's home, until the church was built; it is a smaller version of the font he designed for Sᵗ

Plate 4 Chancel arch murals by Gambier Parry at
The Church of the Holy Innocents at Highnan.

Michael's. Inside the decoration was unrestrained, the walls being ablaze with colour paintings, that is, until they were whitewashed in the 1950s. Today all that remains of this original splendour is the decorated rood screen and a reredos that reaches from the altar to the roofline. Some black and white photographs and an un-whitewashed portion of the wall suggest that the work could have been that of Gambier Parry. If this is so it would have been a very touching gesture on his part. When Woodyer died in 1896, he was buried in the churchyard at St Andrew's, his wife having been buried at Milton, near Abingdon, forty one years earlier.

CHAPTER FOUR

THE OUSELEY FAMILY BACKGROUND

AND

SIR GORE'S CAREER IN INDIA

Perhaps I should next write about the Ouseley family background. The Ouseleys were an ancient family, dating back at least to Thomas Ouseley who lived in Shropshire in 1486. Sir John Ouseley, who, interestingly, was Ambassador to the Emperor of Morocco, was killed whilst fighting with the Spanish against the Dutch at the siege of Breda in the Netherlands in 1624. The family were then living at Courteen Hall in Northamptonshire. Gore Ouseley's pedigree book gives detailed accounts of various branches of the family dating back to the Norman Conquest. In 1625 Richard Ouseley sold the Courteen Hall estate, and emigrated with his brother Jasper to the south of Ireland.

Before continuing with Gore Ouseley's career in India, and especially in the light of Frederick's religious vocation some details of the rather bizarre life of Gideon Ouseley, Sir Gore's cousin, should be included.

The Rev. Gideon (Gridiron) Ouseley.

Gideon was the eldest son of John Ouseley (b.c. 1735) of Kilticoghly, County Galway. He was born at Dunmore, County Galway, on 24th February 1762 at the home of his great-uncle William Ouseley. Gideon's father was an anti-clerical freethinker but his mother was a pious women who introduced him to Anglican and Puritan literature.

Despite his father's anti-clericalism, he decided on a career in the Church of Ireland and was tutored by the local Catholic priest, Father Keane, who had been educated in Europe. It was after he had failed to win a place at Trinity College, Dublin, that he studied with his cousins under Dr. Robinson. In 1781 his father inherited a farm in County Roscommon. Shortly afterwards, in 1783, Gideon married Harriet Wills (1762–1853) of Wills Grove. They had no children. The marriage resulted in a small estate being settled on him by her father. However, the estate subsequently had to be surrendered, probably unnecessarily, after a lawsuit. Gideon then entered a phase of dissolute living, which was dramatically brought to an end by a drunken shooting accident in which he lost an eye and, very nearly, his life. During his convalescence, his wife read to him Edward Young's gloomy Night Thoughts, which, in conjunction with his near-death experience, resulted in a lasting preoccupation with death and eternity. His first experience of evangelical religion was in April 1791, at a Methodist meeting. Thus began a long and psychologically painful conversion during which Ouseley encountered other Methodist itinerants and joined a local Methodist society. He soon decided to become an itinerant preacher, but his work was undertaken as a freelance evangelist because of his suspicion of ecclesiastical institutions and their clergy. In 1797, he and his wife settled in the town of Sligo, and opened a girls' school. However, in 1799, he was invited by the Irish Methodist Conference to be part of a team of Irish-speaking evangelists with a specific mission to the Irish Catholic poor in the wake of the rebellion of the United Irishmen. Ouseley sang and preached, mostly in Irish, to large gatherings of people at county assizes, fairs, market days, funerals, and wakes, in prisons, and outside church services. One of his reports to Dr Coke, the director of the Irish Mission, paints a picture of one of these occasions –

'On Monday we came to Baillieborough. The market people were assembled when we came into the street. We did not alight from our horses but prepared to attack the devil's kingdom which still remained in the town. The Methodists wished us out of the street when they saw the manner of our proceedings, riding on our horses, with our umbrellas over our heads, the day

being wet. A young girl was so alarmed that she feared the Day of Judgment was at hand'.

Gideon Ouseley was not only characterized by his evangelical zeal but also by his anti-Catholicism, which predated his evangelical conversion and was part of a wider anti-clericalism. He drew a distinction between priests and the ordinary people, whom he regarded as victims of priestly tyranny and insupportable financial burdens. During the 1820s Gideon, apart from his continuing commitment to preaching, spent much of the decade publishing his own highly individualistic solutions to Ireland's miseries. His remedies were for more responsible landlordism, a more equitable and rational assessment of tithes, the state payment of Catholic priests, and an electoral register based on minimum educational standards to ensure that landlords would have to provide schools for those over whom they exerted economic and political influence.

Throughout his life he never gave up the battle against Popery. The following article appeared in *The Times* on September 23rd 1833, when he was over seventy years old.

METHODISTICAL STREET PREACHING IN DUBLIN

For the last three Sunday evenings the neighbourhood of the North Strand has been thrown into a state of 'spiritual agitation' by the persevering efforts of the Rev. Gideon Ouseley, a primitive Wesleyan Methodist, who is generally termed by the Catholics "the Rev. Gridiron Ouseley," from the unceremonious denunciations that he indulges in against the "disciples of holy mother church". Having sent round handbills through the neighbourhood, he took his stand on the steps of a hall door belonging to one of the disciples of his congregation, in Coburg Place, on the first Sunday (Sept. 3rd) and delivered a sermon, with prayers and hymns, not at all complimentary to the majority of the crowd which he addressed. (All crowds in Dublin are at least nine tenths Catholic). He was however protected from insults by a phalanx of his friends who immediately surrounded him. On the second Sunday evening he again appeared in the same place. The crowd were more numerous and unruly and their tendency to insult the preacher was not at all lessened by his candid expression of opinion of "the damnable errors of the church of Rome," and the necessary (Gridiron) consequences to its followers. Towards the conclusion, the still increasing mob became courageous; they hissed and hooted, and eventually those on the outskirts threw stones at the preacher and obliged him to take refuge within the house, not, however, without loss of his pocket handkerchief and his hat. The former was carried by the captors on the top of a stick in triumph, and the latter was kicked about by the crowd until it was left crownless and worthless. A small pulpit which the Rev. Gentleman had stood and thumped with great animation, was broken up by the assailants, who shouted victory, and imagined they had silenced the preacher forever. The old gentleman however, with a spirit worthy of John Wesley, appeared again at the same hour, on the same steps, in a new pulpit, and again exhorted the "poor benighted adherents of Popery" to forsake the errors of their ways. This time the crowd, which was even larger, threw mud, potatoes, rotten eggs as well as stones. The preacher eventually had to make his escape, but some of his supporters who interfered to defend him were very roughly handled'.

It shows a perfect example of the turbulence of the times, to recall that whilst the crowd that confronted Gideon Ouseley was very strongly pro-Catholic, the crowd that confronted his cousin's son, Frederick Ouseley, outside St Barnabas' sixteen years later, was very strongly anti-Catholic.

Gideon Ouseley died in Dublin on 14 May 1839 and was buried at Mount Jerome Cemetery, Harold's Cross, Dublin. There is a memorial church to him in Mountmellick, Queen's County, the town in which he preached his last sermon. At the heart of Gideon Ouseley's personality and work were a sincere religious faith and a genuine compassion for his country and countrymen. He was one of Ireland's most influential figures in the early nineteenth century. It must be said however that his *Four Letters*, published in 1829, makes for rather heavy reading.

Gore Ouseley In India

In 1787, at the age of seventeen, Gore Ouseley set out, or was sent out by his father Capt. Ralph Ouseley, to seek his fortune. He travelled first with his uncle, Mr O'Donnell, transporting a cargo of wine from Bordeaux to America, and then via China he made his way to India, where he busied himself in commercial affairs. By 1792 he had settled at Bygonbarree in the Dacca province of Bengal where, along the banks of the River Brahmaputra, he established a factory producing Baftas (fine cloths) which were sold more cheaply than elsewhere in the province. See (Plate 5) He lived a relatively solitary existence and spent his leisure time studying Persian, Bengalese Hindi, Arabic, and Sanskrit. He became an elegant speaker and writer of Persian. In addition to his linguistic and literary pursuits he concerned himself deeply with music, an accomplishment he passed on to his son, Frederick.

In 1794 he made the acquaintance of the eminent orientalist Sir William James who made a deep impression on him. Gore was already actively collecting books and manuscripts, but for the discriminating collector, this was no easy matter. He wrote to his brother that *'Manuscripts, as you have heard, are common in India, and cheap, that is, we consider them so; but not one in a hundred is correct, some are defective, and others are ill-spelt.'* Most of the manuscripts are now in the Bodleian Library, either items that Sir Gore sold to John Bardoe Elliott of the Bengal Civil Service in about 1842 and which Elliott later donated, or the thirty five manuscripts that Sir Frederick sold to the Bodleian in 1858 for £500. Together these form the richest of that great library's Oriental treasures. Having been in the libraries built for them at Woolmers and Hall Barn, Sir Gore's printed Oriental Collection finally came to rest, as a collection, at St Michael's College in the very fine double-cube room which was especially built by Sir Frederick. (See Plate 26). Since the closure of the College in 1985 the whole library has been dispersed; the music items went almost entirely to the Bodleian, but most of the Oriental printed books were sold through the trade. I have managed to acquire fourteen volumes. The Library is now more or less empty. (See Plate 25).

Plate 5 The banks of the River Brahmaputra, painted by Sir Gore when he was 17, and where he established a factory making Bafta fine cloth.

SERVICE IN INDIA

Having lived in various parts of India, Ouseley went to Lucknow, capital of the province of Oude, in 1795. A chance occurrence resulted in him acquiring more insight into and experience of public and political service through his friendship with, and attachment to, Nawab Shuja ud-Daula, Wazir of Oude, as his Major Commandant and Aide-de-Camp. This crucial development in his life in India came about by The Nawab being equally struck by Ouseley's knowledge of Persian (the court and official language of much of India), and of the language and customs of Hindustan. As an officer of the Nawab's personal staff, his translator (closely involved in discussions between the Nawab and the British Government in India), his confidential secretary in matters of Government, and his companion at other times (the Nawab called him his 'best and only friend'), Ouseley was in a very influential position at the Court of Oude.

Anglo-French rivalry in India increased as a result of Napoleon's invasion of Egypt in 1798 when Marquess Wellesley took counter-measures to defend the British position, including a policy of subsidiary treaties with local princes. Within this strategic context, Ouseley earned Wellesley's approval for his well-judged attempts to cultivate good relations between the state of Oude and the British power. This resulted crucially in Wellesley's later furthering of Ouseley's career. Ouseley returned to England in 1805.

CHAPTER FIVE

SIR FREDERICK OUSELEY'S CHILDHOOD

Details of his time in India are fascinating, but Sir Gore eventually settled down a little, and on 12th April 1806 he married Harriet Georgina, daughter of John Whitelocke, an army officer. They had two sons, Wellesley Abbas Ouseley and Frederick Arthur Gore Ouseley, and three daughters, Mary Jane, Eliza Shirin, who died in infancy, and Alexandrina Perceval. Ouseley was created Baronet on 3rd October 1808. In 1809, on the recommendation of Wellesley as Secretary of State for Foreign Affairs, he was nominated mehmendar, guide and host to Mirza Abul Hasan, the Persian ambassador to Britain.

Frederick's father had a very successful career working in India for the British Government for seventeen years. Before Sir Gore and his wife left England in 1810 to take up his appointment as the Persian Ambassador, the family lived at Claramont (See Plate Six). This was a small country house just outside Cheshunt in Buckinghamshire. Claramont was conveniently only about twelve miles from the East India Company College at Hertford Heath where Sir Gore's step-brother, Major Joseph W. J. Ouseley, was Professor of Persian and Arabic. Major Ouseley had previously taught at the College of Fort William in Calcutta during the time that Sir Gore was in India. The East India Company College closed in 1858 and the very fine buildings, designed by William Wilkins, reopened as Haileybury School in 1862. Claramont was sold for redevelopment.

The site of the Ouseley home is preserved by the misspelt Claremont Drive housing estate in Cheshunt. After his successful service in India, Sir Gore became Ambassador to Persia from 1810 to 1814. He then retired and finally returned to England in 1815, rather expected to be

Plate 6 Claramont, Sir Gore's Country House

made a peer. It is believed that he was recommended for a peerage by the Duke of Wellington. However he did receive a civil list pension of £5,000 a year, the equivalent of which today would be over £200,000 a year.

Sir Gore and Lady Ouseley's first son, Wellesley Abbas, was born whilst they were in Persia. He died aged eleven and was reburied at the Church of St. Mary and St. John, the parish church of Hertingfordbury, which is not far from Woolmers, where Sir Gore lived after Claramont. There are two memorial plaques on the south wall of the nave –

The upper plaque reads -

> "Sacred to the memory of
> WELLESLEY ABBAS OUSELEY
> The eldest son of The Right Honourable Sir Gore Ouseley Bart.
> and Harriet Georgina his wife.
> He was born in Tabriz in Persia on the 4th day of August 1813
> And departed this life the 9th day of March 1824,"

The lower plaque reads –

> "MORS LUPI AGNIS VITA
> Near this place lies interred all that was mortal of
> THE RT. HONOURABLE SIR GORE OUSELEY BART G.C.H. Etc Etc
> Several years Ambassador Extraordinary from the Court of Great Britain to
> H.M. The Shah of Persia.
> He was born June 24th 1770 and died November 18th 1844. This monument is erected to his memory by Lady Ouseley, his widow,
> as a tribute of her devoted affection."

The family crest is a wolf's head with a bleeding hand in its mouth, the motto being "Mors lupi agnis vita".

The legend is as follows: "A gallant warrior of that name had married a most beautiful young lady named Agnes, about the time that Edward I., after his return from the Holy Land, marched through

Shropshire to attack the Prince of Wales. Ouseley, being of rank in that county, considered it his duty to meet the King and invite him to his house, though it was with reluctance he left his bride. Agnes on the following day went a short distance to meet the King and her husband, accompanied by her maidens, when as she approached the royal party, a huge black wolf rushed out of a holly thicket and bit off her hand. So intent was the ferocious beast on his prey that the enraged husband was enabled to seize him, strangle him before the King, and sever his head from his body. Before this adventure the Arms of the family of Ouseley were "Or, a chevron in chief, sable," but upon this occasion the King granted the augmentation "of three holly leaves, vert," and added the crest of a black wolf's head excised, with a right hand in its mouth couped at the wrist, gula, on a ducal coronet, with the motto "Mors lupi agnis vita"; and it is said that there existed in a church in Shropshire a monument containing the figures of this warrior and his lady, in which the latter was represented without the right hand".

When Frederick was born, his elder sisters, Mary Jane and Alexandrine, were eighteen and eleven years older respectively. With his abilities and wealth Sir Gore became a figure of some social importance in London. By 1825, Sir Gore was a Fellow of the Royal Society, a Fellow of the Society of Antiquaries and a member of the Privy Council. He was also a member of The Travellers Club, as is noted below. Like everyone else in fashionable society, Sir Gore needed a town house and a country estate to match his status. When he retired in 1815 and came home for the last time, he bought Woolmers, or Woolmer Park (Plate 7), in the parish of Hertingfordbury in Hertfordshire, which was even nearer, only about four miles, from the East India Company College. In 1825 he bought 33, Grosvenor Square, and then in 1832 Sir Gore purchased Hall Barn, near Beaconsfield in Buckinghamshire.

No. 33 Grosvenor Square

No. 49 Upper Grosvenor Street

Frederick Arthur Gore Ouseley was born on 12th August 1825 at 33, Grosvenor Square. He was christened on May 16th 1826 with the names of his two godfathers, H.R.H. Prince Frederick, Duke of York and Albany, second son of King George III, Arthur Wellesley, His Grace the Duke of Wellington, and that of his father. His godmothers were Marchioness of Salisbury and his eldest sister, Mary Jane. He was christened by his uncle, the Reverend Spencer Whitelocke. It could be added that the Duke of York's elder brother became King George IV and his younger brother became King William IV; such were the circles in which Sir Gore moved.

Number 33 Grosvenor Square, where Frederick was born, was leased from the Grosvenor Estate by Sir Gore from 1825 to 1838. The house was on the south west corner of the square, where Upper Grosvenor Street runs into Grosvenor Square. It was the easternmost house, No. 49, on the south side of Upper Grosvenor Street. About thirty feet of the northernmost end of the house faced east into Grosvenor Square, hence the No. 33, but it seems as if the front door was on Upper Grosvenor Street. I have done much research at the City of Westminster Archives Centre, with the kind permission of the Grosvenor Estate, to find the precise location of Frederic's birthplace. One of the problems was that the house numberings in the Square have changed quite a few times over the last two hundred years. Sir Gore's house, No. 47, was on the west side of Upper Grosvenor Street, and No. 34 Grosvenor Square was on the east side. Although No. 34 had the entrance on the square, the property ran alongside South Audley Street. At the rear of all three was Reeves Mews. Sir Gore's house was demolished in 1886, but there is a floor plan of the building in the Westminster City Archives, from it one can begin to see a little of the Ouseley family's lifestyle.

The Grosvenor Estate lease plan for Sir William Smith, 7th Bt. dated 2nd March 1810, who preceded Sir Gore as the tenant of No. 33, is also in the archives. Although the plan is only of the ground floor, the house consisted of almost two buildings, the private quarters to the north of the site and the servants' quarters to the south. They were separated by a garden, with an underground passage linking the two. The ground floor private quarters included two large reception rooms (25ft x18ft and 21ft x18ft), which, possibly on the first floor, were combined together as a ballroom, and an entrance hall with an elegant staircase. There were two other stories above, and also a garret. These would have been sitting rooms, bedrooms, bathrooms etc. for Sir Gore, Lady Ouseley and the three children. At the entrance to the underground passage there are three cellars (each 9ft x 11ft). The servants' quarters consisted of kitchen, pantry and out-houses. Above were two more floors of bedrooms and sitting rooms for the servants. It is impossible to say how many staff there were. At Upper Brook Street Sir Gore employed three man servants and eight female servants. At the rear of 33 Grosvenor Street the floor plan shows a two-storey stable block with stalls for eight horses and a coach house for three carriages. Above, there was presumably a tack room and hay storage, and possibly also one or two more bedrooms. The coach house and doorway opened onto Reeves Mews. The word "mews" originally meant a cage for hawks, especially whilst moulting. Henry V's hawks were kept at the Royal Mews near what is now Charing Cross. In Tudor times the mews became stables and in mid-Victorian times many started to be converted to private houses.

This is the house where Frederick Ouseley spent much of his early childhood. Perhaps his nursery was in the garret.

Sir Gore And His Pianos

Research into the archives of John Broadwood and Sons Ltd, at Finchcocks Musical Museum in Kent, reveal some remarkably interesting information about Sir Gore and his obsession with pianos.

John Broadwood's is the oldest and one of the most prestigious piano companies in the world, so a paragraph on the history would not be out of place. The firm was founded by Burkat Shudi, who had come to London in 1718, aged sixteen, from Switzerland, where his family were craftsmen in wood. He became an apprentice to the Soho harpsichord workshop of Hermann Tabel. In 1828 he started his own workshop. In 1761, John Broadwood came from Scotland to seek his fortune. He found it. He was aged twenty nine and the eldest son of the local village carpenter of Oldhamstocks. In 1769 he married Shudi's daughter, Barbara. Ten years later Shudi retired and handed over the business to his son, also named Burkat, and to his son-in-law, John Broadwood. From around 1700, the pianoforte as an instrument had been developing, and, around 1770, Shudi's harpsichord company had started making the more versatile and popular instrument. By 1784, they were making more pianos than harpsichords.

When the author was a boy at St. Michael's, there used to be a harpsichord in the Library. Michael Hart has very kindly added the information that it was indeed a Shudi-Broadwood, and there was a brass plaque on it stating that it was presented by Broadwoods to The Founder.

Such a customer as Sir Gore must have been well-known to Henry Fowler Broadwood (1811-1893), the principal of the firm. In 1815 Henry's father, Thomas Broadwood, had purchased the Juniper Hall estate, not far from Dorking in Surrey, which included Lyne House, a Grade Two listed early Victorian mansion near Rusper. He bought the estate presumably from the French émigrés D'Arblay, Talleyrand etc. The Broadwood family vaults are at the Church of St. Mary Magdalene in Rusper. In the early nineteenth century the building was in a very poor state, and in 1854 Broadwood's commissioned Henry Woodyer to rebuild it. This was Woodyer's commission immediately before doing St Michael's in 1855-56.

The author has pursued this subject of the Broadwood's country estate as it might answer the intriguing and long standing question as to where Sir Frederick and Woodyer first met. However, the St Michael's Foundation stone was laid earlier, in 1852, so perhaps it was Ouseley who introduced Woodyer to the Broadwoods, rather than the other way round. Sir Frederick certainly knew Henry Broadwood, as they both sat on a sub-committee of the Royal Society in 1866 to establish the problem of perfect pitch, but this was much later.

My research into the archives of John Broadwood and Sons Ltd, at Finchcock's Musical Museum in Kent, reveal the following information about Sir Gore and his obsession with pianos. Firstly, in order to try and obtain the best possible Broadwood piano for his household, he either purchased or hired no less than nine grand pianos between 1827 and 1834, thus:

- On 10th March 1827 Sir Gore purchased Broadwood grand piano No. 11,003.
- On 10 May 1827 he exchanged it for No.11,102.
- Also in 1827, he returned No. 9,435, and, in 1828, he returned No. 4905. On 16th June 1834 Sir Gore hired grand piano No. 13,371, and returned No. 11,102.
- On 20th June 1834 he returned No. 13,371 and had in exchange No. 13,449. On 4th July 1834 Sir Gore finally purchased No. 13,508. This was an expensive model described as a six-and-a-half octave patent, which cost £128. 2s. In today's value this would be about £12,000.

It is difficult to see Sir Gore's logic in all this. However, my eldest daughter Kate, who has very kindly proof-read the book, has suggested that if "FAG" had perfect pitch, and these were early pianos, that none of the earlier ones were quite right. Perhaps trying to please the boy made Sir Gore fussy.

The second fascinating fact that emerged from the Broadwood archives was that every year the Ouseley family, with their pianos, moved from their country estate, Woolmers or Hall Barn, to their town house in Grosvenor Square or Upper Brook Street, and then back again. Although the whole period from 1827 to 1844 has not been researched, it is highly likely that the pattern from 1831 to 1834 was repeated annually.

- On 1st March 1831 Sir Gore paid for one grand piano and a square piano to be taken from Woolmers to Grosvenor Square.
- On 4th July 1831 he paid for them to be taken back to Woolmers.
- On 29th February 1832 two pianos were taken again to Grosvenor Square.
- On 18th July 1832 two pianos were returned to Woolmers.

- In the autumn, Sir Gore purchased Hall Barn and the two pianos were taken there from Woolmers 26th September 1832.
- On 8th March 1833 one grand and one square piano were taken from Hall Barn to Grosvenor Square.
- On 17th July 1833 two pianos were taken back to Hall Barn.
- On 24th February 1834 two pianos were taken to Grosvenor Square, and on 29th July they went back to Hall Barn.
- On 15th and 16th April the pianos were tuned, which is not very surprising considering the man-handling they had received.

All this annual travelling of the family and their pianos seems incomprehensible until it is realised that the London Season started after Easter, and ended mid August. The Ouseleys did what the rest of high society, the *'beau monde'*, did. They went to London for The Season and then back to the country for the rest of the year. The Season was a marriage mart, and Sir Gore had two unmarried daughters.

No. 41 Upper Brook Street

In the Census Return for June 6th 1841, details are given of everyone who was living at 41 Upper Brook Street on that day. Sir Gore's age is given as seventy and Ireland as his birthplace, Lady Ouseley is fifty, Miss Ouseley is thirty, Miss A. P. Ouseley is twenty five and F. A. Gore Ouseley is fifteen. They have three male servants, including Thomas Green age fifty who was the butler, and seven female servants, including Catherine Smith, aged forty five. who was the housekeeper.

'The Morning Post', a London daily newspaper, printed a regular weekly column, 'Fashionable World'. The article for Tuesday, May 11th. 1841 reads 'Grand Ball At The Russian Embassy'. *Last night Baroness Brunow, the lady of his Excellency the Russian Minister gave a splendid ball at Ashburnham House to upwards of 400 0f the leading nobility and gentry. The fete was on a scale of unusual splendour, and may be considered one of the most delightful entertainments of the season. The whole range of saloons were thrown open. In the grand dining-room a sumptuous supper was served up. It is almost needless to observe it consisted of viands and delicacies, the choicest that art and wealth could procure, the wines of the most improved vintage. His Royal Highness the Duke of Cambridge, attended by Major Stephens, arrived at half-past eleven, and was received in the vestibule by His Excellency. His Royal Highness retired at ten minutes to one. The general company included the Duke of Wellington and His Excellency Prince Esterhazy'.* This was followed by a seemingly endless list of Dukes, Duchesses, Lords and their Ladies, senior politicians, and, quite a long way down the list, *'Lady Ouseley and the Misses Ouseley'.*

It was said that, when he retired, Sir Gore had half expected to receive a peerage rather than a baronetcy. Indeed, when he was in St. Petersburg in 1814, having negotiated the peace treaty between Persia and Russia, he had a long interview with Emperor Alexander I of Russia, with whom he got on very well. Afterwards, the Emperor communicated his feelings about Ouseley to the Prince Regent and to Lord Castlereagh, strongly recommending him for a peerage. However, Sir Gore's youngest daughter Alexandra, or Alexandrine, had an even stronger connection with the Emperor of Russia; she was named after him. Alexandra and Alexandrine are Russian feminine forms of Alexander. Lady Ouseley, who had been pregnant whilst she was travelling across Russia with Sir Gore, gave birth when they were in St. Petersburg. At the christening, which was held in the Grand Church in the Winter Palace , the baby was held at the font by her godmother, the Empress of Russia. This is confirmed by an entry in Lady Ouseley's bible. Her other godmother, from whom she received the name Perceval, was Mrs. Spencer Perceval, the widow of the Prime Minister. Mr. Perceval had been assassinated in the lobby of the House of Commons in 1812, the only British Prime Minister to have been murdered.

It has already been mentioned that The Season was a virtual marriage market. Once she had been presented at Court, a girl could expect to attend well over one hundred balls, parties and dinners during a single season. If she did not marry within three seasons and reached the age of thirty, it was thought that she would probably remain a spinster. In 1841 Mary Jane was thirty and Alexandra was twenty five. Obviously Sir Gore, who was seventy one in 1841, was anxious to see both his daughters married, but he died three years later. Mary Jane and Alexandra died, both unmarried, in 1862 and 1861.

The week following the ball at the Russian Embassy, 'The Morning Post' of Tuesday, May 18th reads *'Grand Concert At Buckingham Palace'. The Queen gave a concert last evening at Buckingham Palace. The Grand saloon was fitted up as a music room for the concert, and the yellow drawing room and the picture gallery were also opened. The company began to arrive at half-passed nine o'clock, and were conducted into the picture gallery'.* After listing the names of various members of the Royal Family who arrived about ten o'clock, the article goes on *'Her Majesty and Prince Albert, preceded by the lord Chamberlain and the great Steward entered the saloon soon afterwards, accompanied by other members of the Royal family. The concert then commenced.'* There follows a long list of those who *'had the honour of receiving invitations'*. About two thirds down the list were *'Sir Gore Ouseley, and Miss Ouseley'*. The programme of the concert, which consisted of vocal works, was then printed. Donnizetti, Martini, Mosca and Casca, came before the interval, followed by Haydn, Mozart, Rossini and Schubert. The report on the concert ends with *'The company were served with refreshments during the evening in the green drawing room, and at half past eleven supper was served in the dining room'*.

So here we have the fashionable society, or *'beau monde,'* being entertained by the young Queen and her Consort. When we think of Queen Victoria we see in our mind's eye an image of a stout little old lady, with her grey hair done up in a bun. Nothing here could be further from the truth, and it is so difficult to imagine. In 1841 Victoria and Albert were only twenty two years old, and they had been married for less than a year. She was so very young and he was so very handsome, at least she said he was. However, when she came to the throne, Victoria was not popular. The Royal Family had been tarnished by the four Hanoverian Georges who were seen to be mad, extravagant and remote to the ordinary people. Her marriage to another German prince, who was tactless and very serious, did not help matters. However, as a growing world power, Britain felt strong and confident, and there was a mood of buoyancy in the country. This feeling of optimism surrounded the young monarch, in spite of her Royal predecessors, age and gender. The rather elderly and very gentlemanly statesmen, such as Lord Melbourne and the Duke of Wellington, who surrounded and advised her, bring to mind the ageing, and very gallant, Winston Churchill and the young Queen Elizabeth.

Woolmers

Sir Gore purchased Woolmers, or Woolmer Park, in 1815. (Plate 7). Woolmers had been built by the Duke of Bridgewater, with James Lewis as his architect, from 1796 – 1802. Sir Gore remodelled the house from 1821 – 1823 by adding a long colonnade of Doric columns between two bay windows at the garden front of the house, and also a dining room, an entrance porch and a staircase. The architect was C.R. Cockerell, whose acquaintance he had made at The Travellers Club where they were both members. Indeed they were both founder members. The original idea of the club, by Lord Castlereagh and the other founders, dates from the return of peace in Europe following the Napoleonic Wars. They wanted a club where gentlemen who travelled abroad might meet and offer hospitality to distinguished foreign visitors. The club was established at a meeting in the spring of 1819. No doubt Sir Gore was a prime mover; it would seem to be an ideal involvement for him.

Frederick Ouseley fondly remembered his childhood home in the name of the tune *'Woolmers'* that he composed for the hymn *'They come, God's Messengers of Love'*. This was written for the dedication of the Church of St. Michael and All Angels in 1856, and very appropriately it was sung at Ouseley's funeral in 1889.

Hall Barn

After living at Woolmers for seventeen years, Sir Gore evidently wanted an even larger house for his family, and in 1832 he purchased the Hall Barn Estate near Beaconsfield. Hall Barn (See Plate 8), sometimes called Hall Barn Park, was built for the Restoration poet Edmund Waller

Plate 7 Woolmers, Sir Gore's Country House

in about 1670, and Sir Gore bought the house from one of the poet's descendants. It is an extraordinarily handsome mansion, stately but compact, of three stories with coupled pilasters at the corners and a hipped roof. The capitals on the pilasters are different on each floor, Ionic, Corinthian and Composite, which is most unusual. Sir Gore enjoyed gardening and building work as he had done in India, and over the years the house was considerably added to and altered. Shortly after purchasing Hall Barn, Sir Gore wrote to Sir William Waller asking for information about Edmund Waller, anecdotes and so forth, and also about his armorial bearings. He writes *'Do you happen to know at what period the crest was granted? I am inclined to think that the original crest (I am a tolerable herald) was a walnut tree, proper and fructed.'* He goes on to say, *'Although I am making large additions to the house I will preserve most scrupulously the primitive character of the original building.'* It is a good letter but the response was disappointing. Sir William Waller sent a rambling four page reply which was all about his own ancestry and nothing about the poet or Hall Barn. Incidentally, when Edmund Waller was imprisoned in the Tower of London in 1643 as a result of 'The Waller Plot' against Parliament, Sir John Denham petitioned the King for Waller's life to be saved. Denham argued that *'Whilst Waller is alive, I will not be the worst poet in England'*. I know the feeling.

When Frederick Ouseley lived at Hall Barn as a boy, there was a magnificent reception room called the 'Great Room', which was 30ft. by 45ft. and 30ft. high. This building, which Sir Gore obviously used for lavish entertaining, was detached from the main house, and faced the lake. The 'Great Room' burned down in 1840, perhaps too many candelabra at a large reception. Sir Gore also built a huge south wing on the main house which included a large library and other reception rooms. This whole south wing was demolished in 1969.

It was at Hall Barn that Frederick played the piano, and also sang, for his father's illustrious guests when they visited. Amongst these exciting visitors was Felix Mendelssohn. The story is that they played a duet together, with Mendelssohn suggesting that Frederick extemporised on his part. (Plate 10). The story is well known, but my recent research

Plate 8 Hall Barn, Sir Gore's last home.

Plate 9 The Rt. Hon. Sir Gore Ouseley, Bart. F.S.A
Painted by R. Rothwell, R.H.A

Plate 10 Sir Frederick Arthur Gore Ouseley. Painted in 1837, when Ouseley was 12, by John Lucas

has shown when it actually occurred. The visit must have been between Ascot in June, and the end of the year. This is when the Ouseleys, along with the rest of High Society, lived on their country estates.

On April 13th 1832 the Duchess of Hamilton wrote a letter as follows – *'I have been today to hear Sir Gore Ouseley's little boy, and never was I so affected by anything in my life. I can find no words to express my astonished delight when I saw the little fellow, only six years old sit down to the pianoforte and commence an extemporaneous performance which baffles all description. His large dark eyes lit up, his whole soul seemed intent on what he was about, and yet with all this there was such a genuine childish simplicity. I could not say half of what I felt. Read the accounts of Mozart's infancy and you have read this child's.'*

The following is taken from *'A Memoir of the Late Right Honourable Sir Gore Ouseley, Bart. sometime Ambassador to the Court of Persia'*, by The Revd. James Reynolds, M.R.S.A., Perpetual Curate of St. Mary's Hospital, Ilford, Essex, and Secretary of the Oriental Translation Committee of the Royal Asiatic Society. It was printed in Sir Gore's *'Biographical Notices of Persian Poets,'* 1846.

'Sir Gore Ouseley, although since his return from Persia he suffered from attacks of gout and rheumatism which affected his hands and feet, yet in other respects enjoyed good health. When debarred by these attacks from his favourite amusements of turning and riding, in both of which he excelled, he diverted himself by drawing, painting, emblazoning and illuminating, and many specimens remain which attest his admirable taste and skill in these accomplishments. However during the last two years of his life, a great change was observed in him, especially by his affectionate family, and his strength appeared to fail. On the 30th of October, 1844, he took his last ride, and on the 1st November, after his return from London, where he passed the morning, to his seat at Hall Barn Park, he was attacked by a disease which subsequently proved to be ulceration of the intestines. He grew gradually worse until the 15th when he consented to remain, for the first time in bed. On the 15th his medical attendants announced his approaching dissolution. He survived however for 32 hours in great agony, which he endured with the utmost resignation. He addressed expressions of deep affection and kind farewell to his afflicted family, and

Plate 11 The Library at Hall Barn, built round a magnificent Royal Persian carpet. It was a gift from the Shah, and was brought back from the embassy.

sorrowing domestics, retained sense and consciousness to the last moment, and was so perfectly calm and collected that he even prayed in Persian. His suffering was terminated by death on Monday the 18th November, 1844, in the 75th year of his age.

Sir Gore Ouseley was Grand Cross of the Guelphic Order, and of the Russian Order of St. Alexander Nevski, and Grand Cordon of the Persian Order of the Lion and the Sun. He was succeeded in the baronetcy by his son, Frederick Arthur Gore'. (Plate 9)

After Sir Gore's death, the family's town house in Upper Brook Street was sold. Lady Ouseley, Sir Gore's widow, went to live at Lowndes Street, where she died in 1848, aged sixty one. She suffered from a weak heart.

In 1846 Sir Frederick sold Hall Barn to John Hargreaves, a wealthy cotton spinner and calico printer from Accrington in Lancashire. Hargreaves sold the estate to Allan Morrison in 1872, who bequeathed it to his brother Charles, who sold it in 1880 to the press baron Edward Levy-Lawson. Levy-Lawson's father, Moses Levy, had acquired the Daily Telegraph shortly after it was founded in 1855. He followed his father as managing proprietor and sole controller, and became very influential in Fleet Street. After being created a baronet in 1892, he was raised to the peerage as Baron Burnham of Hall Barn in 1903. The family is still in residence. The author has been helped considerably with research on Hall Barn by the Rt. Hon. Mrs Lucia Whitehead (nee Lawson), the first Lord Burnham's great granddaughter.

Until he went to Dorking to be tutored by the Rev James Joyce when he was thirteen, much of Ouseley's childhood was spent on the family estate. His name says much about his father's social position. There is a delightful picture described by F. W. Joyce of the annual interviews that took place between the gentle home-educated boy with his highly-strung musical nerves and his godfather, the great 'Iron Duke'. It seems it was the Duke who was shy and stiff and awkward, who did not know what to say next, and who appeared more relieved than his godson, when the ordeal was over for another year. As Colles writes "The Iron Duke might well be embarrassed by this strangely impressionable child who could play the Hallelujah Chorus from memory without knowing what it was after hearing it played once as an 'out voluntary' in church" The musical child prodigy anecdotes about Ouseley have been frequently repeated, but he must have been extraordinary. His other godfather, Prince Frederick, Duke of York, died in 1827 which was too soon for him to take any practical interest in his godson. One story, reported by Sir Gorge Elvey, who was organist and choirmaster at S[t] George's Chapel, Windsor, for nearly fifty years, was that Ouseley could tell the notes in a group put down at random with the flat of the hand on the keyboard. Many years later, in 1856, Elvey played the organ at the consecration service at St. Michael's, but, much to Ouseley's disappointment the installation of the Flight organ was incomplete.

The present owners of Hall Barn have a Broadwood grand piano in the Long Gallery, where it would have been when Sir Gore and his family lived there. The author thought that perhaps this was the piano that the young Frederick performed on for his father's illustrious visitors. However the serial number on the piano shows that it dates from 1886. John Broadwood and Sons Ltd have very extensive archives in Kent, including retail sales ledgers.

Plate 12 The Old Rectory in Dorking

Plate 13 Dorking in 1880

CHAPTER SIX

THE JOYCE FAMILY AND DORKING

The Joyce family of Dorking (Plate 13) had a considerable influence on Ouseley's life and development. Evidence of this is acknowledged by Ouseley himself in that no less than three members of the family became Fellows of St Michael's – James Wayland Joyce in 1856, and Frederick Wayland Joyce and James Barclay Joyce in 1894. This is a remarkable record for one family.

The story starts in 1840 when Sir Gore sent the young Frederick Ouseley, aged fourteen, to be tutored for entrance to Oxford by the Rev. James Joyce (1781-1850), Vicar of Dorking. Also living in the Vicarage (Plate 12) were the Vicar and his wife Sarah's five sons and four daughters. James Wayland Joyce (1812-1887), the eldest son, was his father's Curate when he also gave lessons to the young Ouseley who was thirteen years his junior. The two formed a lifelong friendship, which was cemented when Ouseley made Wayland the first Fellow of his new College in 1856.

However, to go back to Dorking, the Vicarage was a very large building, which is just as well as there were a considerable number of people living there on 6th June, the day of the Census. Firstly there was the Vicar, Rev. James Joyce, aged fifty nine, his wife Sarah, aged forty nine, and their son James Wayland, Clergyman, aged twenty eight, four more boys aged twelve, ten and eight, and four daughters aged twenty two, twenty and eighteen. Then there were his pupils -Hugh (surname is indecipherable) aged eighteen, Berkeley Stanhope, aged seventeen, Bernard Howard, aged fifteen, and Lord Ribblesdale, aged thirteen. As these were colleagues of Ouseley, it seemed worthwhile to research a little about them if possible. To start with, Bernard Howard is rather too usual a name, but Berkeley Stanhope is easier to find. There was a Rev. Berkeley Stanhope who was vicar of Weobley in Worcestershire and who attended the Poor Law Conference in Great Malvern in 1875. Then there is Lord Ribblesdale. Thomas Lister, the 3rd Baron Ribblesdale, served in the Royal Household Guards and died in 1876 aged forty eight. One would imagine that Ouseley might have kept in touch with Berkeley Stanhope, but perhaps not with Lord Ribblesdale. There were also two male and five female servants living in the house.

James Wayland Joyce was a remarkable man. His writings show the depth of his learning and scholarship. He wrote at least half a dozen theological works including *'A Constitutional History Of The Convocations Of The Clergy, From The Earliest Records Of Christianity in Britain To The Date Of The Promulgation Of The Present Day Book Of Common Prayer: Including A List Of All Councils Ecclesiastical As Well As Civil Held In England.'* This seven hundred and fifty page weighty tome was published by Rivington's in 1855. He followed this in 1862 with *'Ecclesia Vindicata: A Treatise On Appeals In Matters Spiritual, With Suggestions For Amending The Course Of Proceeding In Appeals from the Ecclesiastical To The Judicial Committee Of Privy Council'*. As I said above, Wayland wrote about four more books in this vein, which seem to me to be worthy of a Doctor of Divinity, and an enormous credit to his father by whom he was no doubt largely taught. After his ordination Wayland became Rector of Burford, near Tenbury Wells. It was he who suggested that idyllic part of England for Ouseley's new school, and although Frederick Wayland Joyce does not specifically say so in his biography, it was probably his enthusiasm and influence that suggested and persuaded his young friend and pupil to go into the Church, perhaps by example rather than by direct suggestion. The two of them did form a lifelong friendship, and it was a friendship with profound depths. Wayland Joyce must have been a very proud and happy man when he set out on horseback from his vicarage at Burford on the morning of Saturday October 4th 1856 to ride through Tenbury and up to Old Common. At the far end of the Common he could see the shining roof of the new church. *'The weather in the early part of the morning had been very stormy and lowering'*, reported the *'The Berrow Worcester Journal'*, *'but as the time fixed for the performance of the solemn Service drew nigh, it cleared up, and a large assemblage of perhaps six or seven hundred persons congregated at the doors of the church, and in the churchyard. The roadway was thronged with the carriages of the resident gentry, and numerous pedestrians trudged onwards, despite the rain and mud, and at imminent risk to themselves in walking, between the alternating lines of carriages going and returning'.* Wayland Joyce made his way through the crowds towards the vestry door. He was going to sing bass in the choir in the Service of Consecration of St Michael's. He must indeed have been a happy man and very proud of his friend and pupil. He had also been present when the foundation stone was laid on 6th May, 1854, as was Henry Woodyer.

The Rev. James Joyce's second son was The Rev. William Henry Joyce. He followed his father as Vicar of Dorking from when his father died in 1850 until 1870. It was during this time that the chancel of St Martin's was rebuilt to the designs of Henry Woodyer, the architect probably being suggested by Frederick Ouseley. The parish had raised money in the 1830s to rebuild the old medieval nave in the Low Church style – a dominant pulpit and galleries between ugly iron pillars, with the medieval chancel being more or less closed off. This was dedicated just before Rev James Joyce became vicar in 1837. In the 1870s, when The Rev. Philip Hoste was Vicar, the parishioners were asked to agree to having the recently built but unpopular Low Church nave demolished, and a new nave and spire built to the design of Woodyer, which completed his rebuilding of the whole church. This shift from Low Church to near - Tractarianism in thirty years was of course replicated across much of England.

The Rev. William Henry Joyce was born in 1827, which makes him twelve when Ouseley first got to know him in 1839/40. I have a letter dated Christmas Eve, 1858 from Ouseley to William which refers to William's collection of autographs. Perhaps this hobby started when they were boys, together living at the Vicarage. As you can see the letter is not that important, but it implies that Sterndale Bennett and Ouseley corresponded together from time to time, and it gives Ouseley's opinion of him as a composer. The letter reads – *Tenbury, Christmas Eve, 1858. My Dear William Joyce, We never correspond – but I hope we don't forget one another. To show you I not only remember you, but your tastes and collections, I enclose a characteristic letter to me for your autograph collection from William Sterndale Bennett, Mus. Doc. Cantab, Professor of Music in that University – favourite pupil of Mendelssohn, and one of the best composers England has produced. Will you accept it? With all good Christmas wishes from Your sincere old friend, Frederick A.G. Ouseley.*

The Rev. Prebendary James Barclay Joyce was the son of Frederick Wayland Joyce who wrote Ouseley's biography, and grandson of James Wayland Joyce. He was Rector of Coreley, in Shropshire, which is only about five miles north east from Tenbury, and near enough to visit St Michael's from time to time no doubt, and to attend meetings of the Fellows. For some time I have been trying to find the initial link between Ouseley and his architect. Where and when did they first meet? Who suggested to Ouseley that he should employ Woodyer for his new church and college? A new avenue of research has shown itself by looking into the lives of other members of the Joyce family.

On June 14th 1853 Wayland Joyce's eldest sister Laura married George Cubitt (1828 – 1917) later to become 1st Baron Ashcombe. He was the son of Thomas Cubitt, who was the leading London builder and property developer of his day. Woodyer never did any work in central London, but when, at the time that Wayland was suggesting to Ouseley a site on Old Common, perhaps he also asked his brother-in-law if he could advise Ouseley on a possible architect.

OXFORD

Ouseley went up to Christ Church, Oxford, in 1843 aged seventeen, as a gentleman commoner. He matriculated on June 9th the same year. He took his B.A. in 1846, M.A. in 1849, B.Mus. in 1850, and D.Mus. in 1854. He became Professor of Music in 1855.

From his collection records, it would appear that he studied the following:

1843, Michaelmas – Heredotus, Cicero, Algebra.

1844, Hilary – Horace, Praelector, Algebra.

1844, Easter and Trinity – Herodutus, Horace Odes.

1844, Abfruit, mortus patri. (Absent, death of father - Sir Gore died on 18th November 1844, and Frederick obviously went home to Hall Barn)

1845, Hilary – Sophocles, Collonus, Theology.

1845, Easter and Trinity - Herodutus, Horace, Theology.

1854, Michaelmas – Exams in Maths and Physics.

CHAPTER SEVEN

ST. BARNABAS, PIMLICO

When Ouseley went to St Barnabas in 1849 it was as a "voluntary curate". There was a time when having a curate showed the importance of the parish, or that the vicar needed an extra pair of hands. That did not apply in Ouseley's case. Being a "voluntary curate" meant that the Bishop felt that this was a good place to train a newly ordained minister, and, more specifically, that the incumbent was a good person to lead the training.

Ouseley gave the tenor bell to the church in 1849. It is inscribed -

To The Glory Of God, Frederick A.G. Ouseley, Baronet,
Candidate For The Sacred Order Of Deacon

At The New College Of St Barnabas

Give Me 1 Ring

Charles and Gorge Mehars, 19 cwt. 3 qrts. 7 lbs, 49" diam. E flat.

This is an extract from *'The Morning Post'* –

EXTRAORDINARY SCENE AT THE PUSEYITE CHURCH OF ST. BARNABAS, PIMLICO. CHURCH OF ST. BARNABAS, PIMLICO.

A scene of the most extraordinary character, calculated to create considerable alarm and excitement, took place on Sunday, during morning service, the recently erected church of St. Barnabas, Pimlico, at which principles and practices having an affinity to Romanism prevail. In consequence of some attempt to interrupt divine service on the previous Sunday, and there being some apprehension that the congregation might be disturbed, or a breach of the peace committed, Sergeant Loom, very intelligent officer of the B division, and two or three constables under him, the whole being in plain clothes, were placed in the church previous to the commencement of morning service. The sittings being all filled, the church doors were closed, and at eleven o'clock the Rev. Sir F. Ouseley commenced the Litany, which was "intoned" in the same way as at cathedral services, the responses being chanted by the choir. At the conclusion of the Litany two huge candles, placed at each end of the altar or communion table, were lighted by persons attired in surplices, and, an anthem having been sung, the communion service was proceeded with, the officiating clergymen being the Rev. G. F. De Gex, the Rev. Mr. Fife, and the Rev. Sir F. Ouseley. When the commandments had been read, and as the collect for the Queen was being commenced, a well-dressed man was seen to leave by one of the side doors in Church Street, between which and the street there is a small court-yard, or space opening into the thoroughfare by a door in a stone wall, the latter of which the person who quitted the edifice left open. There is every reason to believe that the scene that almost immediately followed was premeditated. The stranger had scarcely left the building five minutes when a loud shouting and yelling, with the clamour of many voices, was heard by those within the sacred edifice, and Sergeant Loom and his men rushed out by the door the stranger had taken, and by dint of great personal activity, favoured by the position of the entrance, succeeded in preventing an attack upon the church until the arrival of a large party of the police. Upon the sergeant first issuing from the church with his men he found that some half-dozen of a mob of nearly 200 had entered the door before spoken of into the space between that and the church, when, a most determined effort, they succeeded in closing the outer door, and thus separating those who had entered from the main body, amidst the cries of " We'll have no popery—down with the church—break the door open," and suchlike exclamations. The few persons who had entered as described retreated over the stone wall upon finding the rest of the party cut off, and the crowd increased momentarily until the arrival of inspector Cumming, of the B division, who was upon the ground within a few minutes with a small party of men; immediately followed by Mr. Russell the superintendent of the division, with a fresh body of constables. At this time the mob must have numbered very near a thousand, and consisted of a vast number gentlemen and well dressed persons, the amount being made up by others belonging to humbler grades. There was very strong feeling manifested by many of the well dressed persons present against the proceedings at St. Barnabas, and it required the exercise of very considerable firmness and moderation on the part of the police to prevent most serious disturbance. By dint of persuasion and force the vast assemblage, which was such as temporarily to cause much anxiety for the safety of the congregation and the neighbourhood, was dispersed'.

After all the trouble, both the Rev. Bennett decided to 'get out of town fast'. As it happened, they both went on the continent. Ouseley went to Germany where he heard the choir boys at Dresden singing so beautifully that he was inspired to establish his own choir school. He also commented on how well they spoke. It is difficult to understand this as I would not have thought that his knowledge of German was good enough for him to differentiate dialects. I assume that the Pimlico choirboys spoke with Cockney accents. Nothing is known about his time in Germany. If he kept a diary, it has been lost. The Rev. Bennett later went down to Frome in 1852, followed by Ouseley's sisters, where he became the vicar until his death in 1886. He was responsible for the restoration, virtually a complete remodelling of the church during the 1850s and 1860s to what we see today. Frome Museum has his surviving library, but his daughter was instructed as executor to destroy any other material relating to the church, apart from his sermons.

It would seem that Ouseley' two sisters, Miss Alexandrina and May Jane, also moved to Frome in 1852. It is all rather hazy, but in 1861 they both lived at the Conigre, an area with a few large houses and at St. John's, a small Roman Catholic Church off Cork Street in Frome. A free day-school was opened at Conigre House by Alexandrina in 1852. Mary Jane died first on 26th July 1861, aged fifty four, and Alexandrina died on

6th December 1862, aged forty eight. Their funeral services took place at St. John's.

This obituary appeared in The Dublin Evening Mail, on Saturday December 13th, 1862.

Death of Miss Gore Ouseley

Miss Alexandrina Gore Ouseley died on Monday night at her residence, Conegar House, Frome, at the age of 47. She was the daughter of Sir Gore Ouseley, the distinguished diplomat, and the god-daughter of the Emperor Alexander I, having been born in St Petersburg during her father's residence in that capital, and his Imperial Majesty testified to the esteem in which he held Sir Gore by becoming sponsor to his child. In her father's lifetime Miss Ouseley mixed in the highest society, the late King William IV being a frequent guest at Sir Gore's house. But she and her sister chose lowlier hearths, and for many years devoted their lives to works of charity, and in ministering to the wants of the poor, in comforting the sick, and in educating poor children, sought to perform the mission which their Master had given to them. It is scarcely a year and a half since the elder Miss Ouseley died; and now that her sister has passed away many poor houses will lack their bereavement aid, many a sick person miss their comforting sympathy, and, especially, many a poor child mourn the affectionate ones who supplied their every want. The Rev. Sir Frederick Gore Ouseley (professor of music at Oxford, and founder of St Michael's College, Tenbury) was with his sister during her last hours.

I have read somewhere that she died of epilepsy, as indeed did Sir Frederick, but I cannot find the reference.

CHAPTER EIGHT

LOVE HILL HOUSE

Before he left England for his year on the continent, Ouseley made arrangements for the St Barnabas choir to remain together as a unit. It is not at all clear why they particularly went to Love Hill House (Plate 14) at Langley Marish. Rather oddly it is also only six miles from Hall Barn. Is this a coincidence or did the Rev. Fyffe and the boys go to Love Hill House because it already belonged to Ouseley? When he sold Hall Barn to John Hargreaves in about 1846, did Ouseley perhaps retain some properties on the edge of the estate? An earlier house on the site was demolished and the present building dates from around 1820. The land however was part of Sir Robert Harvey's Langley Park estate and Love Hill House was possibly the house occupied by his agent. In these circumstances it could obviously not have been part of the Hall Barn Estate. Also, in an undated letter to Wayland Joyce, but probably of January 1851, Ouseley writes 'As regards Dorking - Fyffe objects to go so far from London. He is going to take a large house near, but not in, London'. This implies that Ouseley had suggested that the choir might be housed in Dorking. Rev. James Joyce could have kept an eye on them and of course they could have sung in Dorking Church. This was obviously a good idea and the right thing to do. Fyffe's objection about the distance of Dorking from London does not make sense as the distance from Langley Marish to London is about the same. Whatever the reason, by March 30th 1851, which conveniently for us was the date of the Census Return, the Rev. Henry Fyffe and his choirboys were firmly established at Love Hill House.

Plate 14 Love Hill House

The details on the Census Return of the occupants of the house were as follows:

- Henry Fyffe, Head, age 34, Clergyman, Birthplace: Marylebone, London
- Frederick H. Smith, Visitor, age 31, Clergyman, Chiltern, Middlesex.
- John Hampton, Assistant, age 18, Schoolmaster, Pimlico, Middlesex
- Henry Pratt, Prefect, age 12, Scholar, Marylebone, London
- John L. Budinger, Pupil, age 12, Scholar, Chelsea, Middlesex
- Eldred Fennel, Pupil, age 12, Scholar, Pimlico, Middlesex
- Alfred J. Capel, Pupil, age 12, Scholar, Westminster, Middlesex
- John Benn, Pupil, age 12, Scholar, (blank)
- Brinkley, Pupil, age 9, Scholar, Pimlico, Middlesex
- James Dachs, Pupil, age 8, Scholar, Chiltern, Middlesex
- George Tuck, Pupil, age 8, Scholar, Pimlico, Middlesex
- Belinda Gale, Servant, Widow, age 47, House Servant, Ireland
- Mary A. Gale, Servant, age 17, House Servant, Tower Hamlets

Of all the above names John Hampton is the one about which most is known; he was one of Ouseley's most faithful disciples. Hampton was born in 1834 and was a pupil in Mr Davis's private school in Knightsbridge when Mr Bennett, Vicar of St Paul's, came to look for choir boys for his new St Barnabas Church in Pimlico. Hampton was a key figure in training the choir at Love Hill House and later became Sub warden of St Michael's College and then Warden after Ouseley's death in 1889. Five years at Langley, thirty-three years as Sub-Warden and twenty-seven years as Warden all add up to a long and full life of commitment to Ouseley and his ideals. After he retired Hampton lived another six years, and died aged eighty eight in 1922.

He was buried appropriately alongside the grave of the Founder, his friend and mentor.

After Ouseley had been ordained deacon in 1849 but before the church of St. Barnabas was finished the Rev. Henry Fyffe came to help with work in the parish. The two men became lifelong friends. Although the little school at Langley Marish was Ouseley's idea and he paid all of the running costs, Fyffe was the Headmaster, taking all the responsibility of such a position and as a just reward becoming one of the first Fellows of the College.

It would appear that Ouseley's original idea of keeping the St Barnabas choir together was no more than just that. Having started training the choir boys he did not want to disband the group. As stated above, it was while he was on the continent in 1851, hearing German choirboys particularly at Dresden and Leipzig, that the idea of his life's work formulated itself. He was back in England by the end of December 1851, when he wrote in a letter from Love Hill House 'All our old choristers are here, under the superintendence of my late fellow-curate Fyffe, and it is with these materials that I hope to form a nucleus for my projected institution and College'.

Nothing is known about six of the boys on the Census Return but the names of two of them appear again. John Büdinger and Alfred Capel were both aged twelve in 1851 but by 1856 their voices had broken, John was a tenor and Alfred was an alto. Together they were part of the choir for the Service of Consecration of St Michael's, as can be seen in the newspaper report below. How exciting it must have been for the two boys from London, having had five years at Love Hill House to finally travel to far distant Worcestershire to see the glory of Ouseley's new church and to join in the fulfilment of Ouseley's dream. They both continued to live in the area, singing as lay clerks in St Michael's choir. Büdinger took over the local parish school, and his seven year old son is buried in the churchyard. The school was presumably housed in Cadmore Lodge, which was built by Ouseley. John Büdinger was also a skilled calligrapher and the altar missal (Joyce's phrase) he did for St Michael's was said to be very fine. The whereabouts of this missal is sadly unknown. In the 1880s and 1890s Büdinger had a lithograph press at Cadmore Lodge and printed copies of Ouseley's anthems, which he sold.

Alfred Capel later went to Trinity College, Dublin and he became an assistant master at St Michael's. He was later ordained and became a Minor Canon. He is listed as 'Rev. A. J. Capel, Minor Canon, and Vicar of St John Baptist, Hereford.' Ouseley was appointed Preceptor of Hereford Cathedral in 1855, so the two men must have had much in common in the daily work of the Cathedral. Arthur Capel's name appears in the list of subscribers to Havergal's 'Memorials of Frederick Arthur Gore Ouseley', 1889.

It is not easy to imagine the day to day life at Love Hill House, but the picture is fleshed out a little for us by the two last names on the Census Return. Mrs. Gale aged forty seven, who was born in Ireland and was a widow, and her seventeen year old daughter Mary were both described as 'house servants'. Between them they no doubt did all the cooking and the housework. One would assume that the boys made their own beds. Plate 14 shows the original five-bay Georgian building that housed the choir. It is larger than it appears in the photo because there is an extension at the rear which cannot be seen. The two-window extension to the right of the picture was added in 1880. The house with its various later extensions has now been split up into three separate homes. However Love Hill House is still surrounded by fields and the wide open space of Langley Park, much as it was in Ouseley's day.

In his 'Memorials of Ouseley' Havergal includes the following – *'From an Hon. Fellow of St Michael's College - My friendship with our dear friend Ouseley lasted for a great many years and was intimate. But what I know of him is, I fancy, only what is equally well known to the hundreds whose lives were brightened by his unbounded kindness and cordiality. I have a pretty keen remembrance of one occasion when (at Langley) I arrived one snowy evening, after a fatiguing day in London, to take part in a devotional in the Chapel, of the* *entire "Messiah" - nothing omitted, and standing throughout the three parts. It began, I think at 8pm., and certainly did not finish before midnight.'*

It has been suggested that Ouseley perhaps used the manuscript copy of the Messiah that had been used by the composer himself at the first performance in Dublin. This however could not have been so as Ouseley did not acquire the volume for his library until 1867. It was a gift from his friend Edward J. Ottley, one of the first Fellows of the College.

'Then he took us up to his own room, and rubbing his hands, said, "Well, I think we must want some refreshment." The refreshment was strong green tea! Of course, an absolutely sleepless night followed; especially as he room was an exceedingly cold one. At day break, however, I was just drifting into unconsciousness, when a long single file of boys, in their night shirts, passed through the room on their way either to lavatory or oratory, I forget which. The next day was the prize day for the school, but, as might be expected Ouseley was disabled by headache, etc, and commissioned me, a stranger to the place, to represent him and conduct the ceremonies! I well remember, too, the miseries he suffered from the possession of that gorgeous, but perilous, heirloom – the Persian enamelled plate, of pure gold, which he used to hide under his coat and bring down with whispered cautions to show his friends.'

The story of Ouseley's hymn tune *'Woolmers'* is well known, but it is not the only hymn tune that he named after places where he lived. Ouseley wrote the hymn tune *'Langley'* which he set to the words *'O Lord of Health and Life, What Tongue Can Tell'*. This was first printed in The Hymnary, edited by J. Barnby in 1872 and later in Hymns Ancient and Modern, edited by W. H. Monk in 1889. Ouseley also wrote 'Lovehill' to the words *'Far From The World, O Lord, I flee'*. This is in The Anglican Hymn Book, the second edition of 1871, but was first printed in 1854 in Maurice's Choral Harmony. The words of *'Lovehill'* are by William Cowper and were printed in his Olney Hymns of 1779.

After Love Hill House, Ouseley, together with a nucleus of staff and boys, lived at Spring Grove for a short time (Plate 15).

Plate 15 Spring Grove

CHAPTER NINE

BUILDING ST. MICHAEL'S CHURCH AND COLLEGE

The author's original intention was to have Woodyer's plans for the Church and the College, together with the building specifications, as the core of this book. Much can be said about the architectural style of the buildings, Woodyer's earlier and later buildings, and where it all fits into the development of the Gothic Revival (See aerial view Plate 18), but to have had Woodyer's actual building specifications would have been the icing on the cake. The search for the plans has been going on now for nearly five years.

However before writing about the building, we need to write about the site.

Wayland Joyce had become Rector of Burford and had suggested the Old Wood Common area to Ouseley as being highly suitable.

In the event, the St. Michael's parish was carved out of the parishes of Leysters, Middleton On The Hill and Tenbury. This scheme nearly fell through, partly from the natural dislike of anything new which distinguishes agricultural neighbourhoods and fear in the minds of some that Ouseley was a "Puseyite". The then vicar of Tenbury was at first unfavourable to the scheme, but he was dissuaded from this view by the Rector of Burford and the Miller brothers of Bockleton. In 1852 Miss Harriet Rushout died leaving £600 towards the building of the proposed church at the Old Wood. As this money was passed to Ouseley it would have to be a parish church as well as a college chapel.

The two Miller brothers named Thomas and John lived in Bockleton, both clergymen doing duty at Leysters and Bockleton.

Thomas, the elder brother was squire of the Bockleton estate. Both were highly respected locally: old fashioned English gentlemen, both bachelors and thorough Churchmen. John Miller had great ability and was Bampton Lecturer at Oxford and a close friend of Keble.

Ouseley's decision to build his church and college at the Old Wood was initially welcomed by the Miller brothers. But as the building started, the scheme was causing alarm in certain quarters, and creating misgivings in John Miller's mind. In 1856, the elder of the Miller brothers, Thomas, died. A letter from John Miller to Ouseley, dated 13th March 1857, says that at the consecration service many local people were able to see the interior of the church for the first time. It was felt that those living in the locality might like to give something towards the building of the church. Letters were written and a total of £270 was collected and given to Ouseley to go towards the installation of stained glass in the west window. This was the formal letter, but on the next day he wrote a personal letter expressing some of his misgivings towards the scheme. He personally criticises the hyper-ritualism of St Michael's, something totally alien to all the local churches. To quote "We have all along regarded the extent of your plan as a great local mistake: and I would fain express an earnest hope that you will be careful not to damage a good cause by any such form of excess". There are two letters to John Miller from neighbouring laymen: the first writes that he fully supports Ouseley's scheme and encloses £10 for the window fund, the second writer refuses to give anything that would signal his support for Ouseley carrying out the practices and principles of St. Barnabus, Pimlico.

The Bishop eventually gave his consent, and the building went ahead.

It is worth pointing out that amongst all this, something very interesting has come to light. I have found it difficult to estimate the High Anglican nature of St. Michael's when it was founded. There was certainly not much evidence when I was there in the 1940s. It now seems that some objection to the church was centred on Ouseley being a 'Puseyite'. I have always thought that Ouseley had walked away from the Oxford Movement and that the influence of the Catholic Revival on him was minimal. This perhaps was not so. Perhaps in its earliest years St. Michael's was as 'bells and smells' (a phrase I dislike), as the best of them. Perhaps the ceremony at the high altar, all the incense, crossing oneself, genuflecting, candles, processing, asperging, even the Real Presence, were watered down, and that's not the best expression in this context, by successive Wardens, according to their High Anglicanism or otherwise. For High Anglicanism read Anglo-Catholicism if you prefer it.

LAYING THE FOUNDATION STONE

'The Worcester Herald' for 6th May, 1854, gives details of the laying of the foundation stone of the 'NEW CHURCH AT OLD WOOD'. The report reads 'The neighbourhood of Old Wood, being a populous district, and distant from any place of worship, it has been determined upon building a new church for the better accommodation of the resident parishioners on the outskirts of the parishes of Tenbury, Middleton On The Hill, Leyster and Bockleton. The late Miss G. Rushout left £600 towards the building of a church in this locality. We also hear that Miss Rushout is a subscriber to a large amount, and that the land has been purchased and presented by the Rev. Sir F.A.G. Ouseley, Bt. and so far the undertaking has progressed favourably. Wednesday last was the day appointed for laying the foundation stone. The morning was somewhat unpropitious, yet there was a numerous attendance of the clergy and respectable inhabitants, among whom were Archdeacon Waring, Miss Rushout, Rev. Sir F.A.G. Ouseley, Rev. J.W. Joyce, Rev. H. M'Laughlin and family, Rev. Jones, Rev. Adams, Rev. Brown. Rev. T.G. and Mrs Whitfield, A.C. Lowe Esq., George Pardoe Esq., Elias Chadwick Esq., E.H. Owen Esq., F. W. Preston Esq., Wm. Norris Esq., J.L. Sweet Esq., Rev. T.E.M. and Miss Holland, etc., etc. The site is a very advantageous one adjoining the public road from Tenbury to Leominster in the boundary of the former parish, and distant two miles from the town. The architect is Mr. Woodyear, (This is incorrectly spelt, but very interestingly perhaps it shows us how the name was pronounced) of Guildford. The interesting ceremony was performed by Miss Rushout and suitable prayers read by the Ven. Archdeacon Waring, in full canonicals, in a solemn and impressive manner. The following inscription, neatly engrossed on vellum by Mr R. Robinson, of this town, was deposited in a sealed bottle and inserted in the stone; - *"In Nomine Sanctae Trinitatis. Amen. Ad Maiorem Dei gloriam aeternamone nominum satutem, hunc lapidem angulatem Ecclesiae Sancti Michaelis omnianqui angelorum, posuerunt. G.R., F.A. G.O., A.D.V. non Marij MDCCCLIV., Renn x Dickson x Hampden x Eriscopo Herefordens"* ' – (G.R. contractions of Georgina Rushout, F.A.G.O. of the Rev. Sir F.A.G. Ouseley)

Where the foundation stone was placed is rather a mystery. As a Freemason, I always thought it was in the north east corner of the building, but perhaps I am getting confused between the foundation stone and a corner stone. Michael Hart has told me that there is an inscribed cross on a stone on the base of the pulpit. Perhaps Miss Rushout and "FAGO" put the piece of vellum in the sealed bottle in a stone here.

THE RUSHOUT FAMILY.

Miss Georgina Rushout (d. 1900) lived at Burford House, which is situated a few miles from Tenbury, just over the River Teme and in the county of Shropshire.

St Mary's Church, Burford, which is adjacent to Burford House, is a Grade One Listed Building. The church was restored in 1889-90 by the Honourable Georgina Rushout, in memory of her brother George Rushout, 3rd Baron Northwick (1811-1887). The architect was Aston Webb, who also designed Ouseley's tombstone. The Rushouts lived at Burford House; their father was the vicar at St. Mary's. Georgina Rushout was a considerable benefactor of St. Michael's Church. In the article from 'The Worcester Herald' above, it stated that she left £600 towards the building of the church. She also gifted the communion plate and altar vestments, also a portion of the stained glass. The plate consists of two chalices, two flagons, two patens, an alms dish, and two candlesticks.

Plate 16 The Founder's grave.

Plate 17 The proposed clock and bell tower, designed by the architect C.E. Mallows in 1899. He also possibly landscaped the terraces which go down to the cricket pitch.

THE BELL TOWER

In the *'Ecclesiologist'* Vol. XVIII (1857) p.p. 219 to 222, there is an article on the building of the church and the college. It states that, *'The buildings, when complete, will form a quadrangle, the church occupying the whole of the north side, which is next to the public road. The college however will be connected with the church at its eastern and western extremities only by a wall and cloister; for the consecrated ground on the south side of the church will not be otherwise built upon.* (Plate 18). *The church was consecrated last Michaelmas-day, the college-buildings on the east and the south sides of the court will soon be ready for habitation, if they are not so already; the west side is not yet begun. There is no tower or spire, but it is intended to erect a bell-tower over the entrance gateway of the college on the west side of the quadrangle'.*

It did not all work out like that. It is well known that Ouseley overreached himself with his plans, and obviously the west cloister wall and the bell tower were abandoned through shortage of money. Aesthetically the loss of the west wall is probably an improvement; the present view of the whole site, church and college, from the cricket pitch is a constant delight, as is the view from the garth to the cricket pitch and beyond to the beautiful Worcestershire countryside. The loss of the bell tower is a different matter and it is sad it was never built. Oddly enough there is in existence a drawing of a *'Proposed Clock and Bell Tower 1899, designed by the Architect F.C. Mallows'.* (See Plate 17). The position would seem the same as was first intended, near the west end of the church, and it does appear to have an archway entrance, not very different from that of an abbey. How the college trustees, or anyone else, could seriously suggest building a tower in 1899, when money was even shorter than in 1857, is hard to imagine. However there is a document in Ouseley's handwriting named *'Memorandum. St Michael's College. Its Prospects. What it wants. 1858'.* This includes *'To build a Tower and west cloister.... £3,000.0.0.*

THE CHOICE OF NAME.

The reasoning behind Ouseley's choice of name for his church and college is obviously a fascinating one. As we have seen above, the working name of the project was Old Wood Church, from Old Wood Common. In Havergal's 'Memorials of Frederick Arthur Gore Ouseley', (Ellis and Elvey, 1888), in an 'In Memorial' paragraph on p.3, there is the following:

'Ouseley's piety was deeply seated and sincere, but unostentatious; a strong point in it being summed up in the title of a St Michael's day sermon (some years earlier) by his old and intimate friend, the late Rev. A. B. Evans, D. D., 'The interest of Angels in the salvation of men'. It was the hold which this subject had on his mind which led to the beautiful Church and College, which he has left as his memorial, to be called St Michael and All Angels'.

However on this subject, of even greater significance and importance is Ouseley's hymn *'They Come, Sweet Messengers of Love'* he named *'Woolmer's'* in fond memory of his childhood home. He wrote it for the Consecration Service in 1856, where and when it was first sung. It seems it is a popular hymn generally for the Festival of St Michael's and All Angels, but sadly it is not sung these days on Commemoration Day at St. Michael's at Tenbury, perhaps because it is not included in The New English Hymnal or Hymns Ancient and Modern.

THE CONSECRATION OF THE CHURCH OF S⁺ MICHAEL AND ALL ANGELS

The consecration was reported at some length in all the local newspapers. The article in the Hereford Times of 1st October 1856 includes the names of Henry Woodyer as being *'at the Consecration'*, and also of Gambier Parry being there *'in the afternoon.'* One wonders if the two Old Etonians had time to reminisce about their schooldays. The reporter from Berrow's Journal did not include their names.

Plate 18
Aerial view of St. Michael and All Angels' Church
and College

Reprinted from *'Berrow's Worcester Journal, Saturday, October 4, 1856'*

The interesting ceremony of consecrating the collegiate church recently erected at Oldwood (See Plate 18), in this parish, and endowed by the munificence of the Rev. Sir Frederick A. G. Ouseley, Bart., (Professor of Music at Oxford, and Preceptor of Hereford Cathedral,) was performed on Tuesday last by the Right, Rev. the Lord Bishop of Hereford, Dr. Hampden. This rev. gentleman, in a spirit such as animated the good and great men who have adorned those ancient seats of classic learning – Oxford and Cambridge – with so many lasting memorials of their piety and philanthropy, had formed the idea of founding a college for the purpose of affording a liberal education to a limited number of the orphan sons or sons of poor clergymen, and for the encouragement of choral music; at the same time hoping that the sons of wealthier men might in course of time be also sent there for education. A portion of land, situated in a delightfully pleasant and healthy position at Oldwood, distant about two miles from Tenbury, was purchased for the purpose, and thereon are in process of construction the necessary buildings. The college itself will not be completed before next Midsummer, but the church, in close contiguity, having been sufficiently advanced to completion to allow of it being opened for divine worship, was consecrated as above named. The college is intended to receive and educate thirty pupils, and several are already nominated. A portion of the pupils will be maintained and educated gratuitously, in requital of their services in the choir of the church. The Rev. Sir F. Ouseley will be the warden, and he will also be the incumbent of the church, to which a district will be attached.

The site of the church and churchyard contains 2,892 square yards. The church has been endowed with the rents of an estate called Cinders-wood, in the parish of Leysters, Herefordshire, and an annual rent charge has also been assigned for the purpose of its reparation.

The designs for the sacred edifice and college have been furnished by Mr. H. Woodyer, architect, Guildford. The builders are Messrs. Wheeler and Son, of Reading. The church, dedicated to St Michael and All Saints, is of the middle pointed style, and cruciform in plan. It is built of fine rubble masonry, the mouldings, &c., executed in white free-stone. It consists of a choir of three bays, with a polygonal apse, and north and south transepts and nave, with three *large and smaller bays to the west.* There are lean-to aisles to the choir and beneath a lofty clerestory connected by moulded and corbelled arches, with the transepts. The sacristy, or vestry, is on the south side, adjoining the south aisle, a vaulted passage leading from it round the south transept, and into the north nave aisle. There is also a north porch. Excepting the aisles, porch, and vestry, the church is groined and vaulted through in wood. The ceiling over the choir is treated with colour slightly, but over the apse more elaborately. The pavements are entirely composed of Messrs. Minton's tiles, disposed in different patterns more richly towards the east. The altar railing is composed of minute tesserne and geometrical figures. The altar table stands under an elaborate canopy, surmounted with a gift metal cross, on the chord of the apse. The stalls and other choir fittings are of oak, the choir bays and ribs being of wrought iron. A lofty iron screen, with folding gates, divides the choir from the nave, and screens of the same material occur in the double arches leading into the choir. The south transept will be entirely filled by a magnificent organ, by Flight, of St Martin's Lane, the pipes of which will be diapered. The north transept will be used for a baptistery; the font is placed on a cross platform and steps. It is circular in plan and ornamented with foliage, inlaid with green Egyptian marble, surmounted by an oak canopy twenty-two feet in height. Contiguous to the font is a well-executed stone canopy, and an arched recess, with a desk for the registry. The nave will be filled partly with open moveable benches (the railing pierced with tracery), and partly with church chairs. The choir and apse are lighted by two windows filled with stained glass, containing figures of angels (Plate 19); the east window displaying the Saviour seated in majesty, with St Michael kneeling at his feet, with the usual symbols in allusion to the dedication. (see below for photocopies of ten invoices for the stained glass and other items from Hardman's.)

The carving throughout the church is exceedingly bold and good, and the workmanship generally reflects much credit on the workmen employed, and upon the able supervision of the clerk of the works, Mr. Chick. The communion plate and altar vestments were the munificent gifts of Miss Rushout, of Burford House, as also a portion of the stained glass. The plate consists of two chalices, two flagons, two patens, an alms dish, and two candlesticks. The pulpit, of

Plate 19 Church interior

chaste design, is of stone, and is placed on the north side, immediately outside the chancel, and raised slightly from the floor of the nave. It is ornamented with a foliated border, and round it, in canopied niches, are figures of saints and angels. The lectern is on the south sides – a brass eagle with expanded wings. The choir is exclusively appropriated to the officiating clergy, and the choral body. It is lighted for the performance of evening service by eight lamps, disposed four on a side, and seven candles placed in stands on the top of the choir railings. These railings are painted of ultra-marine blue, relieved with gold. The general effect is very imposing. The doors of the sacred edifice are of massive oak, with foliated ironwork.

The weather in the early part of the morning, had been very stormy and lowering, but as the time fixed for the performance of the solemn ceremony drew nigh, it cleared up, and a large assemblage of persons congregated at the doors of the church, and in the churchyard. The roadway was thronged with the carriages of the resident gentry, and numerous pedestrians trudged onwards, despite of rain and mud, and at imminent risk to themselves in walking, between the alternating lines of carriages going and returning. Fortunately, no accident of any kind occurred.

The choir was composed of gentlemen from the Chapel Royal, Windsor, Hereford, Worcester, Gloucester, Exeter, Oxford, and Old Wood College, Tenbury, and clergy connected with the diocese, as follows: -

Trebles – Kirwan, Boardman, Lockyer, Sangster, Caldicott, Corfe, Grounde, Sangster, Butler, Tearon, Kirwan, Caldicott, Arthur Sullivan (later Sir), and Deane.

Altos – Messrs. Capel and Burville, Revs. H.E. Havergal and Sir F.A.G. Ouseley.

Tenors – Rev. John Goss, Mr. Hampton, Capt. Ottley (Fellow in 1856), Rev. – Walker, Rev. H. McLaughlin, Rev. – Norman, Mr. Barnby, Mr. Budinger, Revs. – James, V. Bagne, H. Fyffe (Fellow in 1856), and T. Helmore. Basses – Revs. Dr. Corfe (Fellow in 1888), J. W. Joyce (Fellow in 1856), Wickers, F. Havergal, E. Wellings, - Heartley, and J. Jebb (Fellow in 1856); Sir W. Cope, Bart. ; Dr. Monk; Messrs. F. Hacking, A. T. Crispin (Fellow in 1856), Barnby, Carpenter, and Flight. Was Mr Flight representing the firm of organ builders?

The clergy assembled with the choir in the college, attired in their surplices, where they received the Bishop and preceded him in procession to the western door, where a petition in the usual form was presented to him by the founder, praying him to consecrate the building. His lordship having signified his assent, the choir and clergy moved slowly up the aisle to the altar, chanting the 24th Psalm, "The earth is the Lord's," to a single chant by Farrant. With the exception of a slight unsteadiness in the seventh verse, this passed off well. The clergy and choir having taken their respective positions, the Lord Bishop took his seat on the north side of the communion table, when the instrument of consecration was presented to him by Mr. H.C. Beddoe, who officiated in the absence of the Registrar, which he placed upon the communion table and then delivered the exhortation and afterwards offered up the customary prayers, the congregation (through admitted by ticket filled the church to repletion) kneeling. At the conclusion the Bishop, sitting in his chair, Mr. Beddoe read the sentence of consecration, which was signed by his lordship, and by him ordered to be preserved in the registry of the diocese.

The officiating minister, Rev. Sir F.A.G. Ouseley, then commenced intoning the service. The first lesson was read by the vicar, Rev. J. Chatton, and the second by Rev. G. Gyles. The Venite and proper psalms (84th, 122nd and 132nd) were chanted to Anglican single chants, by Tallis and Purcell; the Te Deum, Jubilate, Credo, Sanctus, and Gloria in excelsis. Rogers in D. major, the précis, vesicles, &c., Tallis. Dr. Elvey, organist of St George's, Windsor, presided at the organ. The anthems, sung after the third collect, and before the Communion service, were "I have surely built Thee an house," (Dr. Boyce) and "Praise the Lord, O my soul," (J. Goss.) The epistle was read by the Rev. E.R. Hampden, and the Gospel by the Rev. F.A.G. Ouseley. The Lord Bishop, after the Nicene creed had been sung, ascended the pulpit and preached an appropriate discourse from the Ephesians, C. 3, V. 10, 11: - "To the intent that now unto the principalities and powers in heavenly places might be known by the church the manifold wisdom of God, according to the eternal purpose which he purposed in Christ Jesus our Lord." His Lordship commenced by observing that the Apostle was speaking of the interest which the angels round the Throne of God take in the salvation of man; they were here represented as rejoicing as its accomplishment – that mystery which, hidden from man in former ages, was

Plate 20 Rev. Sir Frederick A.G..Ouseley 2nd Bt,
by Lewis Carroll (Charles Lutwidge Dodgson, 1832- 1898).
Date: Spring 1860

now made manifest to all nations, and tongues and kindred's of 1people; and the joy consequently felt was described in the text as not confined to the sons of men alone, but was shared and participated in by the angels – those spirits of light and life, who are represented as taking a deep interest in the work of God in the Church. The Holy Scriptures abounded with records of the deep interest taken by the angels in the affairs of mankind, as messengers of mercy, and ministering spirits, and their employment as agents and executants of his righteous judgements. Thus on the fatal day that witnessed the expulsion of our first paten's from their blissful abode in Eden, cherubim and a flaming sword. "kept the way of the tree of life." In the patriarchal and judicial ages, we found them still employed as God's messenger, and so also speaking to and instructing the Prophets. Under the New Testament dispensation their agency was still strongly marked. It was an angel that appeared unto the Blessed Virgin, with the salutation "Hail Thou that art highly favoured – the Lord is with Thee." An angel band appeared to the shepherds with the intelligence of the birth of a Saviour, and inspired the glorious song "Glory to God in the highest, and on earth peace, good will towards men." Was the Saviour tempted in the desert? Invisible spirits were there to attend upon him, and when the Evil One, baffled and defeated, left him, "behold angels came and ministered unto him." They strengthened him in his agony in the garden – and legions of them were ready to come forward and deliver him from the foes who were taking his life. At the sepulchre angels sat, with affectionate care, "one at the head, and another at the feet, where the body of Jesus had lain;" an angel's voice announced the resurrection to the women, and when the Lord ascended in triumph into his Kingdom in heaven, angels announced his return in glory to judge the world. Their watchful service was continued in the time of the Apostles, as evidenced in the cases of St Peter and St Paul, by the latter they were described as "ministering spirits, sent forth to such as shall be heirs of salvation." Such then was the awful pleasing truth which the church laid before them in the services of that day, the festival of St Michael and the holy angels; and which the solemn act of the dedication of that House of God was calculated to impress on their minds. It had been from no merely superstitious feeling that the church had set apart a day for special service in honour of these ministering spirits; not from a feeling akin to that which animated St John, when, overpowered by the sublime *disclosures which an angel was making to him, he was about to cast himself at the feet of the Divine agent in adoration, and was immediately reproved – "See though do it not, for I am thy fellow servant, - worship God;" but mindful of the watchful, loving care which angels are described in the Scriptures as evincing towards mankind, she honoured them for their honour rendered to the Lord, and their sympathy for fallen man. Such was the spirit in which they had that day acted, in consecrating that beautiful House, and separating it forever from all profane and common uses to the glory and praise of Almighty God – and the setting forward the salvation of man. It was dedicated to honour of St Michael and the holy angels. Though nothing they could offer was of itself acceptable to God, in whose sight the heavens were not clean, yet they humbly prayed that he would be pleased to accept that building as an offering of grateful Christian hearts. The right Rev. prelate alluded in graceful terms to the kindness which had prompted the conception of the raising of that building, and to the intrinsic merit of the workmanship; and in conclusion, hoped that the holy exercises in which they had all been that day engaged, would have a permanent effect on their minds, strengthening their attachment to the church and her services, as means of grace.*

At the conclusion of the sermon notice was given of the communion for Sunday next, after the offertory the celebration of the Lord's Supper was proceeded with. The holy sacrament was partaken of by all the clergy present, and a large portion of the congregation.

The service in the church did not terminate till nearly four o'clock. The consecration of the burial ground then took place. The bishop, clergy, and choir, walked in procession round the ground, chanting the 115th. Psalm, to a chant composed by the Rev. Sir F.A.G. Ouseley. The usual forms were gone through and the prayers offered, Luther's hymn being effectively sung by the choir.

The entire of the solemn service of the consecration was not brought to a termination till nearly five o'clock. The bishop and clergy then sat down to an elegant dejeuner which the Rev. baronet caused to be served up in an apartment destined to become the future library of the college. The care of its preparation had been confided to Mr. Groves, of the Swan Hotel, who merited commendation for the manner in which he carried out his instructions. There

Plate 21 St Michael's Church from the north east.

was no speech-making or proposition of toasts, and shortly after the termination of the repast, evening service commenced in the church, which was much crowded. The Lord Bishop was again present. An occasional overture was played on the organ before the sermon, and Handel's admired air "Total eclipse" was rendered as a voluntary after the second lesson, when a collection was made. The prayers were again intoned by the Rev. Sir F.A.G. Ouseley, and the whole service was extremely well performed. The service was Rogers, in D. The anthem by Dr. Elvey, "Praise the Lord, O my soul," was nowise inferior to others of his well-known productions. The sermon was preached by the Rev. John Jebb, M. A., Rector of Peterson, who selected as his text Revelations, c. 5, v. 2. In the course of his observations the Rev. gentleman, alluded to the musical portions of the worship in the Jewish temple, pointing out its divine origin, and showing that it was distinct from the temporary ceremonials of the Jewish polity; and he argued that those who followed the elaborateness and costliness of that ceremonial stood at least on ground than those who betrayed meanness under the pretext of simplicity. They would, as it were, worship Christ in the humiliation and poverty of his manger, but forgot to bring the golden gifts. It was too often overlooked that the Saviour was no longer in humiliation but exaltation, and if in his former state he encouraged and accepted costly offerings, how much more suitable must they now be to his present glorification. He exposed the speciousness of the prevalent cry of utilitarianism, and reminded his hearers they must worship in beauty as well as in holiness. The principal parts of Christian worship he represented as being praise and prayer, and prayer not only as a mere supplication, but an act of sacrificial homage, preaching being a subordinate accessory.

The nave in the evening was lit by groups of candles, suspended from the roof, and the effect was good. The congregation were highly gratified with the day's proceedings. We understand that Mr. J. Hanbury, jun., second son of the Rev. John Hanbury, M.A. Rector of St Nicholas Hereford, has received the appointment of organist to the church.

In the morning a large party of the nobility, gentry, and clergy, partook of the hospitality of Burford House, where an elegant luncheon was provided, and numerous of visitors were staying. Among the clergy and gentry who were present at the ceremonies were – the Right Rev. the Bishop of Hereford and family; Rev. Sir F.A. Gore Ouseley, Bart., Lieut, - Colonel Rushout, M.P. and Miss Rushout; Sir T.E. Winnington, Bart., M.P., and party; Rev. Sir W. Cope, Bart., Sir B. and Lady Leighton; Sir Wm., Lady, and the Misses Curtis; Sir C., and Lady Rouse Boughton and family; Rev. Hugh, and Hon. Mrs. M'Laughlin and family; Rev. Dr. Bowles, Stanton Lacy; Mrs., and the Misses Arkwright; Rev.T.L. Claughton, Vicar of Kidderminster; Mr. E. V. Wheeler, Mrs Wheeler, and friend, Kyrewood; Mrs Wheeler, Newnham Court; Colonel Inigo and Mrs. Jones; Rev. J.Palmer Bromyard; Capt. Capel; Mr J. and Mrs. Freeman, Gaines; Rev. A., Mrs., and Miss Clive Whitfield; Mr. E. Chadwick, Puddlestone Court; Rev. T. E. Miller, Rev. W. H. Havergal, Worcester; Rev. J. Churton, vicar, and Rev. G. Gyles, curate, of Tenbury; Rev. E.R. Hampden, Cradley; Major and Mrs. Lowe, Court of Hill; Miss E. Godson. Messrs A.F. and W. Godson; Mr. G. Pardoe, Nash Court; Mr. T. Ashton, Hatfield; Mr J., Mrs., and Miss Davies; Mrs W. C. Hemming, Ribbesford House; Captain Wellings, Ludlow; Mr. P.P., and Mrs. Williams, and party, Stoke; Mr G. Brown; Mr H. C. Beddoe; Mr. H. Cooke, Wilden; the Misses Cooke, Hill Top; Mr. W. Norris; Mrs. J. Bailey, Eastnor Court, and party; Mr. Andrew Boughton; Mr and Miss Blonni; Revs. W. Poole, W.P. Hopton, D. Melville, E. Wellings, J.J. Hodges, Onibury, T. Vere Bayne, Christ Church, Oxford, T. Elmore, H. Fyffe, J. Buckle, J. Baker, Neen Sollers, G. Marston, T. Powell, G. Scarsbrook, Stanton Lacy, J. Graves, A. Severne, Rock, W. Vernon, E.C. Evans, J. Banks, Ludlow, T. M. Holland, Stoke Bliss, T. Rocke, Exeter, C. Kent, Walcott, G. Pinhorn, W. Poole, T. Underwood, T. T. Lewis, T. H. Hindell, C.W. Landor, Lindridge, C. Whiteford, A. Stonehouse, H.T. Hil, Felton, T. Edwards, Orleton, W. Hulme, J.R. Davies, Knighton-on-Teme, Wm. Pulling, Eastnor; T. Lea, Bewdley Far Forest; W.H. Ricketts, Cleobury; J.D. Williams, Farlow; - Morgan, Witley; Messrs. G. Winton, J. Smith, J. Swann, C.W. Jenner, B. Kenyon, Andrews Grove, Turley, Slade, Farmer, Foster, Roberts, Hancon, Clarke, Baugham, Pound, &c., &c.

The Ven, Archdeacons Lane, Freer, and Waring, and some other of the clergy, were unavoidably prevented attending.

The dimensions of the church are as follows: - Length, 114 feet; chancel 43 feet 6 inches; height 74 feet; width 67 feet. The nave is 22 feet wide (with aisles 45 feet). Accommodation is provided for about 600 persons. The total cost of the church and college, when completed, is calculated to be about

£30,000. *A legacy of £600, left by Miss Rushout, some time back, towards the erection of a new church at Tenbury, has been appropriated, and several of the wealthy residents in the locality have contributed liberally.*

Since Monday choral service has been performed efficiently twice every day, and will be continued to the end of the week, when the choir will be discharged till after Christmas, the building not being completed. Service will be held regularly on Sundays. Those during the week have been well attended by persons far and near.'

Letters to and Invoices of Messrs. Hardman & Co.

The collaboration between John Hardman Jnr. and Pugin was fundamental in the establishment, and indeed the growth, of the world of the Gothic Revival.

Hardman & Co., otherwise John Hardman Trading Co., Ltd., founded 1838, began manufacturing stained glass in 1844 and became one of the world's leading manufacturers of stained glass and ecclesiastical fittings. It was wound up in 2008.

John Hardman senior, (1767–1844), of Handsworth, then in Staffordshire, England (and now part of Birmingham), was the head of a family business designing and manufacturing metalwork. He was described as the 'opulent button maker and medallist'. In the 1830s, Augustus Welby Pugin was commissioned by the Roman Catholic Bishop, Thomas Walsh, to design a suitable church to house the remains of St. Chad, which had been rescued from destruction at Lichfield Cathedral during the Reformation. When the building was consecrated in 1841 as Saint Chad's Cathedral, it was the first Roman Catholic cathedral to be built in England since the Reformation. For the recently converted Catholic, Pugin, this was a commission of great importance.

Pugin first had contact with John Hardman was during the construction of St Chad's Chapel, the forerunner to the cathedral scheme. John Hardman junior, (1812–67), left the family business in 1838 and set up on his own to manufacture ecclesiastical metalwork. Pugin employed Hardman's to provided metalwork for St Chad's Cathedral. Hardman was an enthusiastic donor, giving the rood screen to the cathedral and being recognised for his provision to various charities by the gift of the Hardman Chantry in which John Hardman senior was interred in 1844, and which remained the family burial place.

From 1845, at the urging of Pugin, John Hardman entered the burgeoning industry of stained glass manufacture. He was joined by his nephew, John Hardman Powell (1827–95) who married Pugin's daughter Anne in 1850, and claimed to be Pugin's only pupil. Powell became the chief designer from about 1849, prior to Pugin's death in 1852. The company took part in the Great Exhibition of 1851 in London, exhibiting the great chandelier designed for Alton Towers.

Hardman and Powell collaborated with A.W. Pugin's son, E.W. Pugin, firstly in the design of the funeral arrangements of John Talbot, 16th Earl of Shrewsbury in November 1852. The collaboration between the Hardman firm and the Pugins was to continue after E.W. Pugin's death in 1875 with the later firm, Pugin & Pugin. This collaboration lasted for three generations and was a major influence on Catholic church architecture and decoration in particular and the Gothic Revival in general.

As a result of pushing himself with an quite extraordinary amount of work, Pugin's last years were traumatic. In February 1852, while travelling with his son Edward by train, Pugin suffered a total breakdown and arrived in London unable to recognise anyone or speak coherently. For four months he was confined to a private asylum, Kensington House. In June, he was transferred to the Royal Bethlem Hospital, popularly known as Bedlam. At that time, Bethlem Hospital was opposite St George's Cathedral, Southwark, one of Pugin's major buildings, where he had married his third wife, Jane, in 1848. Jane and a doctor removed Pugin from Bedlam and took him to a private house in Hammersmith where they attempted therapy, and he recovered sufficiently to recognise his wife. In September, Jane took her husband back to The Grange in Ramsgate, where he died on 14 September 1852. On Pugin's death certificate, the cause listed was "convulsions followed by coma". Pugin's biographer, Rosemary Hill, suggests that, in the last year of his life, he was suffering from hyperthyroidism which would account for his symptoms of exaggerated appetite, perspiration, and restlessness. Hill writes that Pugin's medical history, including eye problems and recurrent illness from his early twenties, suggests that he contracted syphilis in his late teens, and this may well have added to the causes of his death at the age of forty.

These letters and invoices all refer to the stained glass, and various fittings for St. Michael's.

24th Sept 1856. Invoice to the Rev. Sir Frederick A. G. Ouseley, Langley, Slough. For St Michael's Church, Old Wood, Nr. Tenbury.

For 24 pieces of Copper Wire guards for 5 East windows of church.	£30 : 3 : 0
For 20 pieces of copper wire guards for Clerestory windows of church.	£8 : 17 : 0

Henry Woodyer Esq.
1859, April 12th. – Invoice to The Rev. Sir Frederick A. G. Ouseley, St. Michael's Church, Old Wood, Nr. Tenbury.
For Old Wood Church.
To a window of stained glass of 6 lights and tracery, being West Window of Church.   £445 : 0 : 0
Subject – The Crucifixion & Last Judgement.

To 16 pcs of copper wire guards for the above window.	£16 : 2 : 6
To a wrought iron frame for above.	15 : 6
3 cases and packing	£ 2 : 5 : 0
Carriage	12 : 6
Fellow's time and expenses, fixing in church	£10 : 4 : 6
	£475 : 0 : 0

Henry Woodyer, Esq.
The amount of this bill to be paid as below

1859 August 20th by cash (Ouseley)	£100 : 0 : 0
1860 March 26th by cash (Ouseley)	£100 : 0 : 0

1860 October 1st by cash (Cope) £ 50 : 0 : 0
1861 March 7th by cash (Cope) £ 50 : 0 : 0
(this is Sir Walter Cope Bt.)
1859, April 12th. – Invoice to A. Trevor Crispin Esq.,
15 Bentinck Square, Manchester Square, London. W.
For Old Wood Church.
For a window of stained glass and light,
Being the East Window of the North
Aisle of chancel. £23 : 0 : 0
For piece of copper wire guard for above. £ 1 : 0 : 0
Part of case and packing 16 : 0
For part of man's time and expenses in fixing above in church.
14 : 0
£25: 0 : 0

1860, September. – Invoice to The Rev. Sir Frederick A. G. Ouseley,   St. Michael's College, Tenbury.
Bill sent to Sir Charles Rouse Broughton, Bart.,Downton Hall, Ludlow.
For St. Michael's Chapel, Tenbury.
To a Clerestory window of stained glass of 2 and tracery.
£43 : 0 : 0
Subject. The Evangelistic symbols of St. Mark and St. John.
To 3 pieces of copper wire guards
For above. £ 3 : 0 : 0
Case and packing 15 : 0
Fellow's time and expenses fixing Above in church. £3 : 5 : 0

Henry Woodyer Esq. £50 : 0 : 0

1865. July 26th. Letter from the Rev. T. Ayscough Smith to Hardman's.
Tenbury Vicarage,
Dear Sir,
Every day lately has found be so fully occupied that I have not written

to you to say how very much I like the three windows you have executed here so soon as I could have wished. At present they are not in the most favourable light for criticism yet even now they please me very much indeed; both in the general treatment of their subjects and in the colours employed.

Will you be so good as to make a Brass Desk for Pulpit with brass rod and screw for raising or lowering the same. I wish it to be perfectly plain in character.

The size of the pulpit so far as concerns the proportions of the desk is as follows. Measurement of top on the flat – 4 ½ ". Radius from which sweep is formed 1ft. 4 ½". No. 7 line of Desk 12 ½" x 11 ½" price   £3 : 5 : 0 on your list would I think be what I would like. I hope you are pushing the gas fittings. I'm very sorry that you should have had any delay about the order, but I daresay contingencies of the sort are not unfrequent.

When you are ready for colouring please to ascertain from Mr Woodyer his wishes.

I am,

Yours very truly,

T. Ayscough Smith.

What would No. 9 Desk be on a plain stand?

1865. November 21st Letter from the Rev. T. Ayscough Smith to Hardman's.

Tenbury Vicarage,

Sir,

Will you be so good as to send me an Altar Desk like number   6 in your Catalogue, which is richly pierced and engraved and costs £5 : 0 : 0. I should also like to have a pair of Flower Vases like No. 1 of Polished Brass 13 inches high, price 28/- each.

I am very much obliged to you for your permission to return   the Alms Dish.

Miss Pardoe for whom you executed the brass and the two windows for the south side of the Chancel is now at home. Will you be so good as to send the account for the same to her. Her address is
Miss Pardoe,
Broad Street,
Ludlow.
I hope you will be able to send the Desk and the Vases to be ready for Advent.
I am,
Yours truly,
T. Ayscough Smith.

CHAPTER TEN

FROM THE NEWSPAPERS

The British Newspaper Archive contains a remarkably comprehensive collection of newspapers, and an equally remarkable search engine. There follows only a few articles, but anyone wanting more should search on the website www.britishnewspaperarchive.co.uk.

<u>1861 – Wednesday, 9 Octoberss – *Hereford Journal.*</u>

<u>St. Michael's College, Tenbury.</u> (By our own Reporter.) We feel much pleasure in reporting the proceedings in Connection with this, the Fifth Anniversary of the opening this church and college. In consequence of St. Michael's day falling this year on a Sunday, the usual festivities were necessarily postponed until Thursday next. The very beautiful church was, of course, crowded even to excess by a fashionable assemblage of the elite of the three adjoining counties. The churchyard attached to the edifice presented lively and animated appearance, such as could scarcely fail cheer the heart of the most grave or desponding person; while the admirer of the picturesque would not fail to enjoy the beautiful scenery of the surrounding country. The numerous equipages of the gentry, the varied and beautiful costume of the gentle sex, of every hue and colour, rendered the effect of the whole scene not only interesting but perfectly dazzling. Excursion trains on the Shrewsbury and Hereford railway were the means of inducing many persons from those towns and the intermediate stations to be present on this festive occasion. St Michael's and All Angels' Church and College is situated in the healthful and salubrious neighbourhood of Old Wood, about two miles from Tenbury, and was erected as no doubt it will be remembered, about five years ago by the munificence of the philanthropist, whose name, from having been

connected with so many undertakings for the benefit of his fellow-creatures, must be familiar to most of us—the Rev. Sir Frederick Ouseley. It has been customary with the Founder, on each anniversary of the foundation, to hold special services commemorative of the event, and to exercise a noble and generous hospitality towards all who chose to do him honour and sympathise with him in the accomplishment of such good work. As we have stated above, the anniversary this year fell on Thursday last. Morning service commenced at eleven o'clock. The clergy assembled in the library of the college, and there put on their robes. In the cloisters the long and imposing Procession was formed, composed of 26 choristers and 22 other singers, both clergy and laymen, followed by a long train of clergy of every degree and rank. On their arrival at the western entrance to the church, the 122nd psalm was sung in procession, accompanied by the grand tones of the organ. The whole service, including the holy communion, was fully choral. Rogers in D was sung throughout with a vigour and precision that is seldom heard or obtained elsewhere. The anthem was sung with equal power and success. " Praise the Lord, my soul," a spirited and noble composition by Mr. Goss, being most appropriately selected for the occasion. The lessons were read by the Rev. Canon Musgrave and the Dean of Hereford. The sermon was preached by the Rev. Thomas L. Claughton, Vicar of Kidderminster and Honorary Canon of Worcester. This excellent discourse was delivered with great earnestness and plainness, and was listened to with the deepest attention by all Present. We believe that, in consequence of general request, the sermons preached in this church on the previous Sunday and on this occasion, will shortly be published. The learned preacher took his text from Hebrews 1, v. 14—"Are they not all ministering spirits, sent forth to minister for them which shall be heirs to salvation."

At three o'clock a dinner was served in the hall of the college, every seat was occupied. After dessert a number of toasts were and very heartily responded to, the healths of The Founder and Headmaster, Rev. C. T. Heartley, being received with utmost enthusiasm. At six o'clock evening prayers were celebrated, when the church was again perfectly filled, and being beautifully lighted with lamps and candles, presented a sight not easily to be forgotten. An Anthem, composed for the occasion by Sir F. Ouseley, was sung after the 3rd Collect, and the Hallelujah Chorus before the sermon. Rogers in D was the service for the evening, and after the sermon the 104th Psalm was sung in unison to the Hanover tune. The prayers were intoned by Sir F. Ouseley, Dr. Jebb, Rev. T. L. Wheeler, and Rev. C. Heartley, and Mr. Colburn very efficiently presided at the organ throughout the day. The Ven. Archdeacon Freer preached from the 4th chapter of St. Paul's Epistle to the Corinthians, part of the 9th verse—" We are made spectacle to the world, to angels, and to men." Adjourning to the College we found that all the necessary preparations for the concert in the Hall were completed, and a numerous company was assembling, every seat being soon filled, and the whole place being literally crammed. Mozart's " Splendente te Deus " was the first piece, followed by an elaborate composition lately written by John Pole, Esq., as an exercise for the degree of Mus. Bac. at Oxford, and was conducted by the author himself. The subject was the Old Hundredth Psalm, ingeniously worked into solos, quartets, and choruses, with organ and piano accompaniment. A madrigal, in 12 parts, by Sir F. Ouseley, was then sung, consisting of three distinct choirs of warriors, minstrels, and bacchanals. A selection from the "Elijah " then terminated the first part of the concert. Refreshments were banded round the hall, and after a pause of some minutes the concert proceeded with one of Beethoven's symphonies, played by the Rev. J. C. Hanbury, with most perfect ease and good taste, the performance of the rev. gentleman being loudly applauded, as indeed it deserved. The programme was a long one. Several songs and glees were then sung, until most of the performers appeared thoroughly fatigued with the arduous duties of the day. But we must not conclude without alluding to an exquisite performance on the flute by Mr. Matthews, accompanied by Sir F. Ouseley on his own grand piano, in a piece by Beethoven, consisting of three movements. The quality of the tone produced by this gentleman, on his silver instrument, was peculiarly mellow and fascinating, and his execution and expression are such as amateurs seldom produce. This performance was rapturously redemanded and acceded to. Midnight was fast approaching when the crowded assembly dispersed; supper being provided for all who required it, in the spacious library. After a day of complete musical enjoyment and festivity, we take our departure, sincerely hoping that this establishment, so important a nursery for the study and practice music and theology, still but in its infancy, may continue to thrive and increase, conferring, as it doubtless will, a real boon upon our national Church. Amongst the audience we observed—Lord Northwick, B. Botfield, Esq., M.P., Mrs. Botfield, Hon. Miss Rushout, G. Pardoe, Esq., and Mrs. Pardoe, of Nash Court, Rev. J. A. Smith and family, of Tenbury Vicarage, Sir T. E. Winnington, Bart., M.P., and Lady Winnington, Stanford Court; Lady and Miss Curtis, Lady Milman and party, Sir Joseph R. Bailey and Lady Bailey, Canon Musgrave, the Dean of Hereford, Archdeacon Blosse, Archdeacon Freer, J. A. Arkwright, Esq. (Hampton Court), Revds. Dr. Jebb, Dr. Bowles, J. W. Joyce (Burford Rectory), Coltmore, J. Whatts, J. King, T. L. Wheeler, T. L. Wheeler, jun., J. Wettings, T. V. Duncombe, J. C. Hanbury, F. T. Havergal J. Gobs (Hereford), C. Allen, J.J. Scargall (Kyre), Hewett (Leyaters), J. J. Miller (Bockleton), H. Connor, W. Poole, E. Wellings, Rev. F. W. Raymond and party, Rev. T. L. Claughton (Kidderminster) and party, Revds. W. F. Powell (Cirencester), T. B. Hosken (Brecon), E. Jacson (Thruxton), Slade Baker (Clifton-on-Teme), John Pole, Esq., Mus. Boc, Tuchwell, Esq. (Oxford), Revds. T. Hensman, C. T. Heartley ; Jabez Jones, Berkleley (Worcester), Burnett (Hereford), Mr. and Mrs. German Reed, Mr. Matthews, Mrs. Wheeler (Newuham Court) and party, E. V. Wheeler, Esq., and Mrs. Wheeler (Kyrewood House), Rev. C. Whitefoord and family, Rev. H. Brown, Mrs. Brown, and Miss Evans (Eastham Rectory), P. P. Williams, Esq., Mrs. Williams, and party (Stoke House), S. H.Godson, Esq., and the Misses Godson (Court House, Tenbury), Misses Wilkinson, Mrs. Howard and party, Mrs. Croome, Mrs. Phillips, Mr. and Mrs. Cranstoun (Ludlow), Mrs. Davies and party, Rev. T. E. M. and Miss Holland (Stoke Bliss), Capt. Otley, Rev. J. and Miss Baker (Milsom Rectory), Mrs. and Miss Baker, Mrs. Whitcomb and party, Mrs. Cursons, Mr. and Mrs. Preston and party, Mr., Mrs., and Miss Sweet, Mr. and

Mrs. and party, Rev. E. T. Bowden and party (Rochford), Rev. Hubert M'Laughlin, Hon. Miss M'Laughlin, Mr. E., Mr. F., and Mr. R. MacLaughlin, Rev. C. and Miss Landor (Lindridge). Captain and Mrs. Hotchkiss, S. Barber, Esq. (The Jewkes), Mrs. Barber and party, Rev. D. Jones, Mrs. Jones, and party, Mr. Home and party, Mr. and Mrs. Ward (Leominster), Mr. Toogood, &c.

1882 – Saturday, 7 October – *Worcester Journal*

ST. MICHAEL'S COLLEGE, TENBURY. The twenty-sixth anniversary of the consecration of this beautiful church and college was commemorated on Friday last, St. Michael's Day, and the services were continued on Sunday. As is usual, there was a large gathering of clerical and musical friends at the college, who delight to join in what is probably the most perfect form of Divine Service to be found in this country. The order of service was as follows : — Holy Communion, 8 a.m.; Matins, 11.30, processional (Psalm exxii.), Service, Ouseley in F. The first lesson was read by the Rev. Ayscough Smith, vicar of Tenbury ; the second by the Very Rev. Archdeacon of Ludlow. The preacher was the Bev. Martin H. Ricketts, M.A. Evensong at 6 p.m.; service, Smart in B flat; The first lesson was read by the Rev. T. L. Wheeler; the second by Canon Burfield, of Leicester. The preacher was the Rev. G. W. Kitchin, M.A., hymn after sermon, 243. The prayers in the morning were intoned by the Rev. the Warden and Founder, Sir F. Ouseley, Bart. The organ accompaniments were exceedingly well played by Mr. Claxton, and supplemented by a band of strings. In the anthem a new tenor solo was introduced by the composer, Mr. L. Colborne, organist of Hereford Cathedral, which was well sung by Mr. Anstice. There were large congregations at both services. The customary banquet was afterwards held in the College Hall. The evening concert was unusually brilliant this year, owing in some measure to the splendid violin playing of Mr. T. Lloyd-Harries and the fine piano playing of Sir F. Ouseley and Mr. Parratt, the newly-appointed organist of the Chapel Royal, Windsor.

1889 – Friday 12 July, *The Gloucester Citizen.*

THE LATE SIR FREDERICK OUSELEY. A meeting of the committee and friends of St. Michael's College, Tenbury was held yesterday at the Westminster Palace Hotel, under the presidency of Sir John Stainer. The college suffered material loss through the death of Sir Frederick, who devoted at least £35,000 to the church of St. Michael's, and during the 32 years the college had in existence expended no less a sum than that on its maintenance. On the motion of the Rev. J. Hampton, seconded by the Rev. Dr. Miller, it was resolved, in consideration of the lifelong services which Sir Frederick Ouseley rendered to the college, that a sum of not less than £10,000 be raised towards the endowment of the college as the best form of memorial to Sir Frederick Ouseley. On the motion passed an executive committee was appointed to carry out the foregoing resolution. The Earl of Mar, who was elected a member of the committee, spoke of the value of the life work of Sir Frederick Ouseley, and said that for himself he should give the scheme, pecuniarily and otherwise, all the support in his power. At the close of the meeting the Warden announced that up to the present they had received £1,470, result which was very encouraging for the future.

1889 – Saturday, 21 September

DEATH OF Dr. LANGDON COLBORNE. The death of Dr. Langdon Colborne, organist of Hereford Cathedral took place on Monday morning, the news coming as great surprise to a large number of his friends. He was in attendance at the Musical Festival two weeks ago and apparently in his usual health. Here, however, he caught a severe cold, and though death is not directly attributed this, it resulted from a disease from which he has suffered for some time, which was greatly intensified as a result of the chill. The deceased gentleman was born on the of September, 1833, and thus expired directly after he had completed his 51th year. As far as is known none of his relatives partook themselves to music as a profession, but the bent of the lad, who afterwards became a Doctor of Music, was easily discerned. His early training was received under Mr. George Cooper, of St. Pauls Cathedral, and he also attended the Royal Academy of Music. Mr. Colborne succeeded Sir John Stainer as organist at St. Michael's College, Tenbury, the institution founded and maintained by Sir Frederick A. Gore Ouseley. He occupied this position for seventeen years, and on leaving there went for short time Beverley Minster. At the death of Dr. Townsend Smith in 1877 he was appointed to the position of organist at Hereford Cathedral, and ex-officio conductor of the Triennial Festival. It is rather a singular coincidence that his predecessor, Mr. Townsend Smith, died suddenly after returning from Gloucester, whither he had been to attend a rehearsal of music of the Festival. Dr. Colborne entered on his duties at Hereford about the 23rd September. 1877, and, therefore, held the position for 12 years, within a few days. The deceased, as a private man, was of a very retiring disposition and, it is said, often shrank from the publicity which the publication of his works entailed. He composed several Church services and anthems, and at the last Hereford Festival produced a short cantata entitled 'Samuel.' He was married.

1908 – Thursday, 7 May – *The Aberdeen Journal.*

As is well known, Sir Walter Parratt, M.V.0., the newly-appointed Professor of Music in Oxford University, is an enthusiastic chess-player. On one occasion, at St Michael's College, Tenbury, he undertook to play two men in consultation, and at the same time play on the pianoforte from memory pieces selected by those present from any of the classical writers for that instrument. He not only played brilliantly during the games but conversed animatedly with several persons, who did their best to distract him. The game lasted an hour, and Sir Walter was the victor. His pianoforte selections while the game was in progress came from Bach, Mozart, Beethoven, Mendelssohn, and Chopin.

<u>1927 – Saturday, 30 July – *The Yorkshire Post*</u>

VICAR'S SUDDEN DEATH. The Rev. William Abbott Renwick. Vicar of Smallbridge, Rochdale, fell dead Brake Street, Rochdale, yesterday. Mr. Renwick. who was 52. graduated from Hertford College. Oxford, which was Scholar, and took Holy Orders 1900, when was second muster at Grantham School. From 1902 to 1916 was head master of St. Michael's College, Tenbury, and then became Curate St. Andrew's, Manchester, and Master the Cathedral Choir School. He was appointed to Smallbridge three years ago.

<u>1901 – Thursday 4 April – *The Cornishman.*</u>

DEATH OF SIR JOHN STAINER. A telegram, received at Oxford on Monday, announced the death Sir John Stainer, at Verona. Sir John Stainer, the famous musician, was born London in 1840, his father being the schoolmaster of St. Thomas's, Southwark. He was educated at St. Paul's Cathedral choir school, and from there went to Christ Church, St. Edmund Hall, and Magdalen College, Oxford, where he took his M.A. degree. He also passed Mus. Doc. Oxford and Durham and was granted the order of D.C.L. and Hon. Fellow of Magdalen College. He has been a most popular organist and officiated at various times at the churches of St. Benedict and St. Peter, London, St. Michael's College, Tenbury, Oxford University, Magdalen College, Oxford, and St. Paul's Cathedral. His great gifts were universally recognised and he was elected vice-president of the Royal College of Organists, an Hon. Member of the R.A.M. and member of the council of the R.C.M. In 1888 he was created a knight and was appointed inspector of music to the education department. His works are many, and varied in character, and exceedingly acceptable. He was also an extensive writer and edited " Carols Old and New," and a Dictionary of musical terms. He possessed an extensive and interesting musical library, containing old English song books, and old psalm-books and hymnals.

CHAPTER ELEVEN

OUSELEY AND ELGAR

The question of whether Ouseley and Elgar ever actually met is not very clear, but if they did it would have been in the following circumstances when they were both taking part at a concert, Elgar playing the violin and Ouseley singing alto. In 1870 the Rev. John Hampton, the Sub-Warden, founded the Tenbury Music Society, whose concerts were held at the Corn Exchange, which is still standing just off Teme Street, down a roofed passageway. It was Ouseley's custom from time to time to bring his choir down to Tenbury from St Michael's to join with a choir of local people in performing large scale musical works. Elgar and perhaps one of his brothers would sometimes come over from Worcester to play in the orchestra. On 1st July 1885 the concert was a performance of Ouseley's *'The Martyrdom of St. Polycarp'*, with the Rev. John Hampton conducting; Ouseley sang the alto solo, and it is more than likely that Edward Elgar, who played the violin, and his youngest brother Frank, who played the oboe, were in the orchestra on that night; their names are printed on the back of the programme. (See Bland pps. 80, 81) Ouseley was a mature sixty, firmly established in his beloved College, but with only four more years to live, whilst Elgar, who had not yet met his future wife, was a violin teacher and struggling composer of only twenty eight, with not much to his credit and unsure of his career's direction. Age was not the only division between them. In 1931 Elgar wrote about the Worcester Three Choirs Festival of 1878, in which he played second violin, *'We had been accustomed to perform compositions by Sir Frederick Ouseley, and others of the organists and professors of music who furnished meritorious works for festivals, but they lacked that feeling for orchestral effect and elasticity in instrumentation so obvious in the works of French, Italian and German composers'*. It other words, he found Ouseley rather provincial, as indeed he himself was, but at least his sights were set on higher things, i.e. the full orchestral richness of Wagner and Brahms.

I advertised some time ago in a Tenbury newspaper for St Michael's memorabilia. Amongst the replies was a letter from a lady who lived in Tenbury, saying she had about eight early photographic plates. She kindly allowed me to borrow them to get prints done, but sadly would not let me buy them. Amongst them was Plate 27 showing what I now know to be the members of the Tenbury Musical Society Orchestra. Elgar and his brother Frank are not on the photo as they were *'Ladies and Gentlemen who have assisted in the T.M.S. Concerts, but Not Members'* as it says on the back of the programme. The photo shows the twenty-seven members, and their names are given beneath. However it is not easy to see precisely who is who. John Hampton and W. Claxton, the Leader of the Band, can be picked out, as can John Stainer, Walter Parratt, Carl Budinger and William Colbourne.

Now, here is a coincidence. I had been writing about this some years ago, when two days afterwards, I went to a lecture and concert at the Barber Institute to mark Elgar's connection with Birmingham University. The Chairman who introduced the lecturer mentioned that they were honoured by the presence of one of Elgar's relatives, which very much surprised and intrigued me. During the interval I made a point of finding the Chairman and I asked him who the relative was. He said that Hilary Elgar, a great-niece of the composer, was there and in fact she was in the green room just behind him, having coffee with the lecturer and other V.I.P.s. With some trepidation, I walked in and, having complimented the lecturer, who was the music critic of The Times, on his talk, I asked him to point her out to me. Hilary Elgar was the easiest of people to talk with, and I felt very moved at being, in a sense, as close to the great man himself as I was ever likely to get. She told me, amongst other things, that she was the granddaughter of Elgar's youngest brother Frank, whom, she said, played the oboe! She later also told me that the name was pronounced with a long *'a'* as *Elgaar,* and not *Elger,* as one so often hears these days.

I am grateful to the late Dan Symonds, the good friend of many of us and an enormous supporter of everything to do with St. Michael's, for telling me about the following. This Smyrna episode is not only a fascinating anecdote in the Elgar/Sinclair relationship, but it is also relatively unknown. Rather surprisingly, even the Elgar Museum had not heard the story before I mentioned it, and they have asked for details for their records. Among the Ouseley and College archives at Hereford Cathedral Library, there are two box files containing the photographs and correspondence of M.F. Alderson and H.C. Colles with material for their book *'History of St Michael's College, Tenbury'*. Among other items there is an envelope containing a piece of card to which is attached a sprig of dried wormwood. On the card is written in Elgar's hand – *'In memory of FA Gore Ouseley, brought from St Polycarp's tomb above Smyrna for GR Sinclair by his friend Edward Elgar. Sep. 30.05'*. On the envelope Elgar has written *'Dr Sinclair: E.E.'* and *'Craeg Lea'*, which was Elgar's house in Malvern. The card also has on it two bars of music which have been identified by Sir Percy Hull as the *'Fellowship'* theme from the *'The Apostles'*. How Elgar happened to be at Smyrna, in the eastern Mediterranean in the autumn of 1905 is an interesting story in itself. Lady Charles Beresford, the wife of Admiral Lord Charles Beresford, Commander-in-Chief of the Mediterranean Fleet, had invited Elgar and a few others, including Frank Schuster, as guests for a month's cruise. Lord Beresford's flagship was the battleship H.M.S. Bulwark but his guests travelled in rather more comfort in H.M.S. Surprise, which was a despatch ship used as a fleet scout. Lord Beresford was second cousin, twice removed, of Charles Beresford, who was at St Michael's 1952 to 1957.

The invitation came about in this way. From 9th September 1905 Elgar had rented Castle House in College Green, Hereford, for the duration of the Three Choirs Festival. Amongst his house guests was Frank Schuster who was a wealthy patron of the arts and a devoted friend. Over dinner on September 11th Schuster mentioned his invitation from Lady Charles Beresford to a Mediterranean cruise, and the next day the invitation was extended to Elgar. These were heady days for

Elgar. On 11th September he rehearsed the *Introduction and Allegro for Strings,* which was to have its Three Choirs premiere during the festival; the first performance had been in London in March. In the morning of 12th September he was given the Freedom of the City of Worcester by the Mayor, Hubert Leicester, who was his childhood friend. When he emerged into the sunshine from the Guildhall he was wearing the Doctor of Music robes and hood which he had received from Yale University only two months earlier. As the procession made its way along the High Street towards the Cathedral, Elgar looked up to a window above the shop where he had lived as a boy. There, looking down, was his eighty-four year old father who was not well enough to leave his room. Elgar saluted the frail old man as he passed. The following day he conducted the *Introduction and Allegro* at the evening concert, and on 14th September, his father's birthday, he conducted *The Apostles* in the Cathedral. After three days of indecision and dithering about whether he should go on the cruise or not, he eventually made up his mind and on 15th September he left on the 2.45 p.m. Worcester train for London.

The details of the cruise are of little importance to these notes, except that on 29th September H.M.S. Surprise docked at Smyrna in Turkey, which is now known as Izmir. The following day Elgar, with two friends, did some sightseeing in a carriage. They went through the town and then up to the fortifications, and there suddenly was the tomb of St. Polycarp. It is impossible to guess what Elgar's thoughts were. His mind must have been full of the last few days, the honour of receiving the Freedom, the procession through the streets, the face at the window, the civic service in the Cathedral with Sinclair at the organ, and the festival. Suddenly seeing St. Polycarp's tomb must have taken him straight back twenty years to Ouseley's oratorio, the Tenbury concerts with his brother Frank, and his earlier days. His train of thought must have been Polycarp - Ouseley – St. Michael's – and Sinclair, who had been a St Michael's chorister, and breaking off a sprig of wormwood from a shrub near the tomb, he took it back to for him as a souvenir. When Elgar put it in the envelope, the two bars of music which he wrote on it, the Friendship motif from *The Apostles*, was probably still in his mind. The concert on his father's birthday was the last music he heard before leaving England. The martyrdom of St Polycarp around 265 A.D. seems to have been the first known martyr's day to be commemorated. Polycarp, who was the venerable Bishop of Smyrna, was burned at the stake *'on the second day of the beginning of the month of Xanthicus, a month in local Greek calendar, the day before the seventh kalends of March, on a great Sabbath, at the eighth hour'*. An eyewitness report also says, that as he walked out into the centre of the Roman amphitheatre where the stake had been set up, he heard a voice saying *'Be strong, and play the man'*. No one else heard the voice except the few Christians present. We will now skip a few centuries to the Marian Martyrs of the English Reformation. When the venerable Bishop Hugh Latimer walked to his death from the Oxford prison with Bishop Ridley on 16 October 1555, he famously said *'Be of good comfort Master Ridley, and play the man: we shall this day light such a candle by God's grace in England, as shall never be put out'*. At one time I thought the phrase *'play the man'* was rather odd, and out of place. It sounded a bit incongruous, like Victorian muscular-Christianity sentiment and reminiscent of Henry Newbolt's *'Play up , and play the game'* from his poem *'Vitai Lampada' 'There's a breathless hush in the close tonight, etc'*. Then, when I read about St. Polycarp, I realised that Latimer was in fact giving Ridley a covert and veiled message of encouragement to take comfort and be strong to the end, like St. Polycarp.

The eye-witness of the St. Polycarp's martyrdom goes on to record that the bishop's bones were taken away and interred in a place *'where the Lord will permit us to assemble and celebrate his martyrdom – his 'Birthday' – both in order to commemorate the heroes who have gone before, and to train and prepare the heroes yet to come'*. Well, yes, exactly so.

I have gone into the St Polycarp story at some length, and one wonders why Ouseley chose this particular subject for the doctoral 'exercise' for his Oxford Doctor of Music award. It was first performed in 1855 at the Sheldonian Theatre in Oxford. I do not know where Ouseley obtained the libretto, but I was keen to see if the story of the 'voice' was included. My friend John Brown kindly sent me a copy of the libretto and at first I could not find what I was looking for.. However, immediately before Polycarp is questioned by the Roman Proconsul, The Angel (Contralto) has a Recitative *'Thus saith the Lord, the Lord of Hosts: Be strong, Polycarp, and quit thee as a man'*.

On the Smyrna episode there remains only to mention Elgar's *'In Smyrna'*, an atmospheric piano piece inspired, according to Northrop Moore, by dancing dervishes whom he saw in the mosque, an endless line of camels being led through the bazaar by a donkey, the overall heat of the hot sirocco wind and so forth. I have listened to it many times on a CD and I certainly cannot hear any dancing dervishes; it is a gentle and quiet melody that if you play it often enough does become atmospheric. It is the sort of thing you can imagine him extemporising on the piano on H.M.S. Surprise after he had had a hot and exhausting day. This is exactly what he did, and the short piece was printed later in 1905 in *'The Queen's Christmas Carol Book'*, a charity publication of the Daily Mail. It would have been exciting to find that Elgar had used some musical quotation from Ouseley's oratorio in *'In Smyrna'*, as a sort of compliment, but to me at any rate, the two works have absolutely nothing in common.

There was a later connection between Admiral Lord Beresford and Elgar. In 1917 Beresford suggested to Elgar that he set Kipling's four songs *'The Fringes of the Fleet'* to music. Elgar dedicated them to Beresford and they were first performed at the London Coliseum on 11 June 1917. Having first agreed, Kipling then objected; he disliked his work being turned into musical entertainment and stipulated that after the two weeks run at the Coliseum, there were to be no further performances. Elgar said *'He is perfectly stupid in his attitude'*.

CHAPTER TWELVE

BOOKS AND LETTERS

THIRTEEN BOOKS BOOKS FROM ST. MICHAEL'S COLLEGE LIBRARY

Because these books were a part, albeit an extremely small one, of Sir Gore's and Sir Frederick's libraries they are highly valued as Ouseley association items, and the description of them is therefore given in some detail. They are from my collection.

1. Ouseley, Sir Gore, Bt. – (Manuscript) - 'The Badges, Devices, Cognizances of the Kings and Queens of England'. 3 ½" x 4 ½". This fascinating little book, 16mo., has the following inscription on the free end paper - *'This is entirely in the handwriting of my Father, Sir Gore Ouseley, Bart., and the drawing also is entirely his. Frederick A.G. Ouseley'.* The binding is contemp. half ruby morocco, gilt, marbled boards, gilt edges and the title 'Badges of England' on the spine in gilt. Alternate pages have 42 hand painted crests of the Kings and Queens of England from Henry II to James I. Sir Gore gives some heraldic background to each crest and quotes his authorities on page 2.

Heraldry was one of Sir Gore's many interests. In his retirement he spent some considerable time researching the Ouseley genealogy. In 1832, after he had purchased Hall Barn from Sir J. Walter Waller, Bart. who was a descendant of the Restoration poet Edmund Waller, Sir Gore wrote to Walter Waller concerning the heraldry of the Waller family. He was particularly interested in the crest on their coat of arms, and in the letter by way of explanation he says *'I am a tolerable herald'*. Obviously this book *'Badges of England'* was originally at Hall Barn, and maybe Sir Gore painted it on one of the tables in the Library which he added to the house. I purchased this book in 1990 when some books from the S[t] Michael's Library first came on the market. I felt that the dissolution of the school and its great treasures had all the finality and wretchedness of the Dissolution of the Monasteries.

Apart from an interest in heraldry it should also be remembered that Sir Gore enjoyed water-colour painting. (See Plate 5)

2. Bridge, Rev. B. – 'A Treatise on The Elements of Algebra'. (T. Cadell, London, 8vo. 7th Ed., 1831, Three-quarter brown leather with marbled boards). With the bookplate of 'Gore Ouseley Esq'. with 'Frederick Arthur' in FAGO's handwriting above his father's name. Inscribed 'Frederick A.G. Ouseley, from his old friend and Tutor, W. Watson. 1838'. From the Library of St Michael's College.

F. Wayland Joyce writes in his biography that Ouseley went to Dorking to be educated by the Rev. James Joyce 'in February 1840 or earlier'. The inscription in Ouseley's own algebra book of 1838 would indicated that if he was given the book when he was at Dorking Vicarage, he was there before February 1840, but if he had received tuition from Mr Watson prior before to going to Dorking then it would obviously have been when he was still living at home. The family moved from 33 Grosvenor Square to 41 Upper Brook Street in 1838.

3. Butler, Samuel, - 'A Sketch of Modern and Ancient Geography.' (Longman, Rees, Orme, Brown, and Green, London, 9th Ed., 1830, three-quarters black leather with marbled boards). With the bookplate of 'Gore Ouseley Esq'. with 'Frederick Arthur' in FAGO's handwriting above his father's name.

The above two books are somewhat of a pair. They have both been rebound, perhaps at the same time and probably well-worn through schoolroom use.

4. Ouseley, Rev. Sir Frederick A.G. Bt., - 'The Morning and Evening Service together with the Office for the Holy Communion, Set to music for eight-part chorus and solo voices, with accompaniments for a full orchestra and organ'. (Novello, Ewer and Co., 1884.) Musical score, pp. 184, folio, (overall 372 x 278mm.), twentieth century dark blue polished calf, the backstrip with five raised bands with gilt fillet and rope tooling, gilt lettering and repeated decoration, the sides with double gilt fillets, the upper cover with the gilt arms of 'Collegium Sancti

Michaelis', a bookplate of Sᵗ Michael's College, Tenbury and prize inscription dated 1924 to E.G. Ensor, marbled endpapers, a few scuffmarks, good A note on the front endpaper states that this book was 'Given to Sᵗ Michael's College, Tenbury Wells by Mary Ensor in 1966 and was bound on the instruction of R. Fellowes, Director of Music at Windsor & bound by the Queen's binder.'

The S.M.C. bookplate, which is dated Mid Summer 1924, states that the prize was for Music (Theory), and is signed by H.D. Statham. Heathcote Statham was Organist of the College from 1919 to 1926. It is also signed by E.H. Swann, Warden from 1917 to 1936. The 'Queen's Binder' mentioned in the note on the free end paper was Ernest Day, Head Binder of the Royal Library at Windsor in 1966. There is a shelf mark 'KK. lV. 1' on the title page. R. Fellowes, Director of Music at Windsor.

5. Bumpus's copy of Ouseley's Collection of cathedral Music. Mss. notes by John Bumpus. Shelf mark 'KK. 1V. 6'

6. Ouseley, The Rev. Sir Frederick A.G., Bart. – 'Cathedral Music, Services & Anthems, set to music by' – (J. Alfred Novello, London Sacred Music Warehouse, [1853]) pp. 248, Folio. Captain Edward J. Ottley's copy, with his bookplate inscribed 'N.B. This Collection contains the six Anthems composed for me at Rome in 1851 by Sir F. O. – (signed) E. J. Ottley'. With numerous photos and, cuttings and notes. There is a paragraph in Bumpus's handwriting and signed by him which states 'Sir Frederick Ouseley attended Morning Service at St. Paul's - the only time I have ever seen him – on Sunday November 22ⁿᵈ 1885. The Services were Wesley in E and Hoyle in D. He sat in the Minor Canons stalls on the Decani side next to me. I shall never forget his enjoyment of the Service. J.S.B. Shelf mark 'KK. 1V. 7'

7. Bumpus copy of Ouseley's Anthems with numerous (about 22) items and insertions. (13 ½" x 11 ¼") Mss notes by Ouseley and Bumpus. On front paste-down endpaper. Bumpus's bookplate. Newspaper article on FAGO's death, dated in pencil April 1889. An leaf from a tree stuck in, and beneath it - *'From the grave at St Michael's College, Tenbury, Sept 18. 1898.'* Portrait of FAGO, and beneath it, in ink.

'Nat: Aug: 12: 1825. Ob: April: 6: 1889' Brief newspaper obit. Bookplate of Glazebrook family crest. On front free endpaper. 'Ex Dono' and beneath a brief obit written in Latin. Beneath that there is a manuscript sonnet as follows –

- April 6 : 1889 –

Gone! Ere we could again have grasped thy hand;
*   Gone! And no words of parting have been said;*
Gone to that land, that silent land;
*   Gone by the path we all shall have to tread!*

Oh! Why so soon, so suddenly summoned,
*   From friends and noble Art and work for God!*
How much of that sweet Art which thou hast loved
*   Lies buried with thee 'neath the daised sod!*

Nay, say not so! God's servants serve Him still
*   In better ways than we could ere devise.*
And who shall say what angel-voices thrill,
*   What harmonies are heard in Paradise?*

*   Rev. Wm. Wood D. D.*
*   Canon of Christ Church, Oxon.*

In Memoriam: Frederick A. Gore Ouseley.

On the next page there is a letter on St Michael's College notepaper, crest in blue.

Tenbury, Oct. 1st, 1888.
Dear Sir,
I am glad you like my Anthem "One thing". It can be procured from Mr. J. C. Budinger, our Parish Schoolmaster, who lithographs it, and has the copies. If you like I can send you one for your kind acceptance. It shall go today or tomorrow. Believe me, Yours faithfully, Frederick A. Gore Ouseley.

Below the letter is another poem –

> *For now is life a lucid story,*
> *And death a rest in him,*
> *And all is bathed in light and glory,*
> *That once were dark and dim:*
> *And I said –*
> *O thou, who dost my soul deliver,*
> *And all its hopes uplift;*
> *Give me a tongue to praise the Giver,*
> *A heart to prize the gift.*

Also on the page I have stuck another leaf which I picked up near the grave. I am not sure what either of these leaves are.

At the back of the book is the programme for the 45th Dedication Festival, 1901. A copy of the FAGO photo of him in his mortar-board. I have dated it 'possibly 1858'. A photo of the Rev. John Hampton, Second Warden, 1889 – 1917. A photo of the Fellows of SMC. Taken in July 1916 after a Special Meeting to elect a new warden. A newspaper article on the Fifty-First Dedication Festival in 1907. The booklet used at the Consecration Service, 1856. This is in very poor condition. Michael Hart gave it to me; he found it in a ditch many years ago. My book plate and a photo of me laying a wreath on the Founder's Memorial in the church, Michaelmas, 2012. In the photo are also Kate and Rev. Andrew Walters the last Warden of the College. And a long newspaper article *'Analyses of Celebrated Anthems'*, n.d.

The volume consists of four Ouseley Anthems, 'Give thanks O Israel', 'In Jewry is God known', 'Let all the world in every corner sing', 'One thing have I desired'. On the title page of each FAGO has written *'John S. Bumpus Esq. from the Composer, Oct. 1888'*.

8. Sir Gore's copy of Pugin's *Normandy Architecture*. Shelf mark 'V. 11. 16'. I feel that this book is particularly interesting. Maybe when it

was in the Library at Hall Barn, the young Frederick took in down from the shelves one day and became fascinated, even spellbound, by the late 12th century Gothic architecture. Maybe the beauty of the soaring wonder of the high arches and the grandeur of the arcades, for instance The Church of St. Ouen in Rouen, inspired him later to try and replicate it in the Gothic Revival style of his College.

9. Memorials of Sir Frederick Arthur Gore Ouseley, Baronet, M.A., Doctor and Professor of Music in the University of Oxford; Precentor and Canon Residentiary in the Cathedral Church of Hereford; Founder of St. Michael's, Tenbury, and First Incumbent of that Church, by Rev. Francis T. Havergal, D. D., Prebendary of Colwall, in Hereford Cathedral, and Vicar of Upton Bishop. Printed by London: Ellis and Elvey, 29 New Bond Street, W,. Walsall: W. Henry Robinson, Steam Printing Works. Hereford: Jakeman and Carver, and Joseph Jones. MDCCCLXXXIX. Ernest Havergal's copy, with his inscription on the half title. *'Ernest Havergal, with kind wishes from his aunt, J. Miriam Crane. For 1891, Lynwood, Weston-Super-Mare, Dec. 31st, 1890. Presented to the Library of St. Michael's by Henry Havergal, July 1953.Another copy is on the open shelves.' Shelf mark 'N. V1. 44'*

Loosely inserted is a letter as follows:
From Henry Havergal to the Warden.
July 8. 53. 9 Kingsgate Street, Winchester. Winchester 3605.
Dear Warden, Some time ago I promised Harold Shaw that if I came across the old copy of this book, I'd send it to St Michael's. I found it in a very dilapidated state among my mother's things and have had it rebound. I can't imagine that its of great historic or literary interest, but I can see that there ought to be a copy in the Library: anyhow I've known this copy of my father's (nephew of F.T.H.) all my life. Yours, Henry Havergal.

10. Mona's Isle by T.J. Ouseley. Printed by Woodfall and Kinder, Angel Court, Skinner Street, London. John Davies, High Street, Shrewsbury. 1853. Inscribed *'The Rev. Sir F. Gore Ouseley Bart. With the author's compliments.'*

11. The Works of Dr Campion's Works, Edited by A. H. Bullen. Privately Printed at the Chiswick Press. 1882. A. H. D. Prendergast's

copy, with his bookplate, and signed on half-title A. H. D. Prendergast, 7 February 1899.

12. Haydn, Joseph – 'The Creation'

13. Fellowes, Rev. Edmund Horace – 'The Family & Descendants of William Fellowes of Eggesford', Fifteen F.A.G.O. Autograph Letters – previously unpublished.

LETTERS

There are thirteen FAGO autograph letters, and an interesting one from Sir Arthur Sullivan, also two from Sir Gore detailed below –

1. From F.A.G.O. to William Joyce, (son of the Rev. James Joyce of Dorking, and brother of Ouseley's friend Wayland.) On SMC notepaper with embossed college seal uncoloured.

> *Tenbury, Christmas Eve. 1858.*
> *My dear William,*
> *We never correspond – but I hope we don't forget one another. To show you I not only remember you, but your tastes and collections. I enclose a characteristic letter to me, for your autograph collection from Wm. Sterndale Bennett, Mus. Doc. Cantab. Professor of Music in that University – favourite pupil of Mendelssohn, and one of the best composers England has produced. Will you accept it? And with all good Christmas wishes from,*
> *Your sincere old friend,*
> *Frederick Gore Ouseley.*

This letter is also printed in Chapter Six.

2. From F.A.G.O. to Lady Burrard, (possibly widow of Admiral Sir Harry Burrard, died 1820, and Lady-in-Waiting to Queen Charlotte). FAGO refers to her as 'Cousin', and mentions 'my Cousin Frederick Lushington'. Of course FAGO was a great authority on the organ and travelled the country advising on Cathedral after Cathedral as to what was best for their requirements). On SMC notepaper with embossed college crest in green.

Tenbury, March 23th, 1865.

Dear Lady Burrard,

I have been from home, or I should not have allowed your letter to go so long unanswered – I hope you will excuse the unintentional time delay. I return herewith Walkers specification and estimate. I like it very much only I would have suggested the propriety of preparing for an additional stop or two on the Pedal. But that would cost but little. It is a great pity that your available funds do not permit the completion of the Swell-organ at once – but of course that is a matter which can be remedied at any time.

I shall probably not be in London till the time of the Handel Festival at the Crystal Palace, but I shall be delighted then to look after the organ at the Factory.

I seldom go from home unless for business – but if I should chance to come your way, I will not forget your very kind invitation. Pray give my very kindest remembrances to my cousin Frederick Lushington who is always associated in my mind with my very earliest and pleasantest recollection, and Believe me,

Your affectionate Cousin,
Frederick Gore Ouseley.

3. From FAGO to the Dean of Ch: Ch: , Oxford. On SMC notepaper with embossed college crest in blue.
Tenbury, Feb.8th, 1870.
Dr Mr Dean,

Many thanks to you for your letter – also to the members of your Chapter for supporting my book. Most assuredly the Anthems it is to contain will be very useful in Choir – I venture to predict that some of them will become <u>great favourites</u> for they show a power of melodic expression that is astonishing in so early an English composer, I have put <u>new words</u> to some of the Anthems, to fit them for use - of course I have recorded the old words in a note, but they consisted of toadying flatteries of James I, such as could only excite laughter. I thought therefore the adaption of possible words to the notes would not be deemed an editorial outrage. I mention this to show you what pains I have taken to render the book useful in Choir – I will therefore take you at your word, and *put down the Dean and Chapter of Ch: Ch: for twelve copies, and this will also enable me to print a prospectus with names of subscribers which I would not do until I knew how my work was supported at Oxford. I did not know that you had not had already had Chapter meetings, and therefore I fear I must have seemed impatient in writing to Bayne, but the fact is I was impatient to get out a Prospectus, for it will be a dead loss to me if I cannot secure at least 200 names – I have now only 156, but I am very hopeful. I have recently found an old organ book of about Gibbon's date which supplies many missing elements in my work, a most fortunate thing as regards completeness, but inasmuch it makes the book larger, it increases my expenditure proportionately, and therefore enhances the need of subscribers.*

With renewed thanks,

Believe me,

Yours very truly,

Frederick A. Gore Ouseley.

4. From F.A.G.O. to Mrs Selwyn. (She was the wife of George Augustus Selwyn. 1809-1878. First Bishop of New Zealand, 1841, and from 1867 Bishop of Lichfield. The Synod of New Zealand was collecting tunes for its own first Hymnal). On SMC notepaper with embossed college crest in purple.

Tenbury, October 26th. 1877.

Dear Mrs Selwyn.

You are quite welcome to any tune of my composition, in any way or at any time, so far that is as the copyright is mine.

I can assure you that I have not the very pleasant time at Lichfield with you, and it will give me very great pleasure to come again to you some day, if you will receive me, as you so kindly say.

With best regards to the Bishop.

Believe me.

Frederick A. Gore Ouseley.

P.S. I only got your letter late last night on my return from Oxford.

5. From FAGO to Mrs Alderson. (She and Mr Alderson were the parents of Montague F. Alderson. They sent their son to SMC as a boy in 1878, so he was one of 'Ouseley's boys'. I remember him well. In this group of letters there is one from him to me dated December 30th 1955. He was my link, as it were, with the Founder. Ouseley certainly knew about Broadwoods – see the paragraph in Chapter Six on all the Broadwoods Sir Gore tried out at Hall Barn when Sir Frederick was a boy). On SMC notepaper with embossed college seal uncoloured.

London, May 9th 1879.

My dear Mrs Alderson,

I have today tried a number of pianofortes at Broadwood's, and I have marked two as being the best for the same money, each costing you £80 nett, and I told Broadwood's heal manager, Mr. Rose, that you would write to him and say which one of the two you would prefer. One is a very fine oblique trichord cottage, while the other is small sized horizontal cottage grand. You will do well with either, and if you write and tell Mr Rose which it is to be, he will at once forward it to you.

Believe me,
Yours very truly,
Frederick A Gore Ouseley.

6. From FAGO to Dear Sir, (an unknown recipient. Dr Charles John Corfe, 1843-1904, was obviously one of the Examiners. He was the first bishop of Corea, and a Fellow of the College in 1884.) On SMC notepaper with embossed college seal in blue.

July 1st 1880.

Dear Sir,

We have passed your exercise, and you will receive it back from Dr Corfe in a day or two.

The October examination will commence on the 12th.

I am,
Yours Faithfully,
Frederick A.G.Ouseley.

7. From FAGO to Dr. Longhurst. (William Henry Longhurst, 1827-1898, was organist of Canterbury Cathedral for very many years. He was organist at St. Michaels 1886-1889.) On SMC notepaper with embossed college seal in purple.
Tenbury, October 20th, 1886.
My dear Dr. Longhurst,

    We have elected Mr. Lancaster to be Organist at St. Michael's College and Church. I forgot whether I wrote to tell you so before. I hope it may not be long ere he comes to enter on his duties, as at present I am "between two stools".

    Let me take this opportunity of repeating my invitation, and saying how much I would like to show you my Musical Library here. If you could come anytime between this and January 1st I should be delighted to see you, and I think I could make your visit pleasant to you.

    I much regret that I have not been able as yet to come and hear your new organ. Are you quite satisfied with the Electric action? I have a particular reason for asking that question.

    Believe me,
    Yours very sincerely,
    Frederick A.G. Ouseley.

8. From FAGO to unknown recipient.
(In the event Sullivan's 'Golden Legend' was performed at the Three Choirs festival in 1887). On SMC notepaper with embossed college seal in blue.
Tenbury, December 1st. 1886.
My dear Sir,

    I have first to apologise for my delay in answering your letter of 26th. I have been very busy, and also from home, so that my correspondence has fallen in arrears. I hope you will, on that ground, kindly excuse me.

    As regards Hodson's 'Golden Legend', I will mention the matter, but I greatly fear that they will prefer to do Sullivan's, nor can I well go against it, if it be so, because Sullivan is a great personal friend of mine, and I have known him from his boyhood intimately, consequently I should not like to be arranged

Plate 22 The Founder in 1883.

against him, or his work – but if his work is not chosen, then I will do what I can for the other. It is only right to add however, that although I am Canon and Precentor of Hereford, and a member ex – officio of the Committee of the Festival, yet my influence therein is not great, whether from jealousy or some other cause, I know not, but last time I received such a rebuff as I shall never forget. It has well-nigh determined me to have nothing more to do with the festival! So I do not expect much good to come from my advocacy at Hereford.

    Believe me,
    Yours very truly,
    Frederick A. G. Ouseley.

9. From FAGO to unknown recipient. On SMC notepaper with embossed college seal in pale blue.
Tenbury, January 28th, 1887.
Dear Sir,

    I am sorry to say I have no separate drawings of ancient instruments, and I cannot well send you copies of bound books out of our Library here, excepting Naumann's History of Music, which I forward herewith. This will supply most of what you want. I would also recommend you to consult Dr. Stainer's 'Music of the Bible'. I would have sent you that too, but my copy is at the Binders.

    I am,
    Yours faithfully,
    Frederick A.G. Ouseley.

10. From FAGO to Canon Robeson. On notepaper embossed in black with the Ouseley crest with the motto 'Mors Lupi Agnis Vita'.
The Close, Hereford. August 18th. 1887.
My dear Canon Robeson,

    Your letter has just reached me here. I am sorry to say I cannot possibly come to you at Tewkesbury on Sept. 27th as it will be the last day of my residence here, and I have some difficulty in getting a brother Canon to take the three remaining days of the month for me, so as to enable me to be at St Michael's College for my Commemoration Festival there on the 29th. September, and the following week. This however I Think I can now accomplish, but you will see at once how utterly impossible it will be to anywhere else at that time. Perhaps at some future time you will let me come and see you at your noble Abbey Church again, instead.

With kind regards to Mrs Robeson,
Believe me,
Yours very truly,
Frederick A. G. Ouseley.

11. From FAGO to Fred (otherwise unnamed recipient. Presumably if FAGO says there is no other, he is referring to the Lewis Carroll, 'Alice in Wonderland'– Charles Lutwidge Dodgson – photo). On SMC notepaper with embossed college seal in purple.

Tenbury, January 10th, 1888.
My dear Fred,

I do not know of any other photo of myself other than the one enclosed. But possible Jones of Ludlow may have taken one. It were worthwhile to enquire there.

I'll "do my possible" as the French say, to choose you a pianoforte when I go to London. You may trust me for that.

In haste,
Yours affectionately,
Frederick A.G. Ouseley.

12. From FAGO to Wharton. (an Oxford examiner.) On notepaper embossed in black with the Ouseley crest with the motto 'Mors Lupi Agnis Vita'.

The Close, Hereford. July 13th 1888.
My dear Wharton,

We have never yet so much as examined a lady in music at Oxford at all, nor do I believe they can graduate in it at all, although they may be examined.

Surely if ladies take degrees they should be termed Spinsters and not Bachelors?

I am now in Canonical Residence here till Michaelmas, and if you are coming in this direction shall be delighted to show you all hospitality – don't forget!

Believe me,
Yours very sincerely,
Frederick A.G. Ouseley.

13. From FAGO to 'old friend'. On SMC notepaper with embossed college seal in blue.
Sunday,
My dear old friend,

It did me good to see your handwriting today. It will do me still more good to welcome you here in propria persona.

I shall however be in Convocation from the 3rd to the 7th of July so come on the 7th and stay as long as you can. We break up on thr 20th July.

I cannot write more today as I am suffering from a terrible headache, and must lie down between Services.

Yours Ever Affectionately,

(Delightfully signed with a music rebus with his initials as the notes F – A – G on a treble clef surrounded with the O of Ouseley).

14. From Sir Gore Ouseley to an unnamed peer. On single sheet.
Woolmers, July 17th 1822.
My dear Lord,

I did not receive your summons for Friday last, but got your letter of Monday yesterday and consequently in full time to have enabled me to meet you today at Sir John Murray's but that unfortunately it is the day on which my Lords the Judges dine with the Lord Lieutenant (Lord Salisbury) and to meet whom Lady Ouseley and I have been invited an age ago. The Dinner hour (4' o'clock) is also such that is I did not run up to town to meet the sub-committee I must have left it before it was well met. May I therefore beg the favour to give me a line by the post to say what day next week you propose having another meeting and I will take care to be in my place at an early hour? Tomorrow and Friday and probably Saturday I shall be engaged with the Grand Jury and Judges at Hertford, but after that I am entirely at your order, but let me have a line tomorrow.

I will try and do what I can in the way of subscription today – en attendant you'd have the goodness to put down Lady Ouseley's name as a candidate for the office of Visitor.

I really am quite delighted with your plan and have little doubt that but that it will succeed and flourish, which will be a proud desideratum obtained.

Yours most sincerely,
Gore Ouseley.

15. From Gore Ouseley to Clarke (an unknown recipient, possibly the secretary of the Royal Asiatic Society.) On folded sheet with the address on it. Mr Clarke Esq., Royal Asiatic Society – ineligible word – 14 Grafton Street. Remains of the wax seal.
41 Upper Brook Street, Saturday.
Dear Clarke,

It was my intention to have attended your summons for this day, but the shock which my spirits have sustained from the death of my dearly loved friend totally incapacitates me from meeting you today, on what I conceive may be the melancholy subject of your deliberations.

You will greatly oblige me by sending me a line of information after the meeting.

Yours sincerely,
Gore Ouseley.

CHAPTER THIRTEEN

FELLOWES / COLLES, PINE / SYMONDS

Edmund Horace Fellowes, Henry Cope Colles,

George Edward Pine and Dan Symonds.

Brief biographies of these four men have been included for the simple reason that a book on St Michael's would not be possible or imaginable without them. The first two were important in their respective fields. To me as a twelve year pupil they were impressive guests of the Warden when they followed after him, processing into the Dining Hall for meals. Edward Pine, or Pinny as he was known, taught me English and memorably about Tarka the Otter. Dan was a good friend of mine.

Edmund Horace Fellowes

Edmund Horace Fellows C.H., M.V.O. (11th November 1870 – 21st December 1951), was a Church of England clergyman and musical scholar who became well known for his work in promoting the revival of 16th and 17th Century English music.

Fellowes was born in Paddington, London, on 11th November 1870, the fifth child of Horace Decimus Fellowes, assistant director of the Royal Army Clothing Depot, and his wife Louisa Emily, daughter of Edmund Packe, a Captain in the Royal Horse Guards. Fellowes showed musical ability at an early age. When he was eight years old he received an offer from Joseph Joachim to become his violin pupil, the offer was not taken up and, later, Fellowes went to Winchester College. He studied as an undergraduate at Oriel College, Oxford from 1889 to 1892, taking a fourth class in theology and becoming a bachelor of Music and Master of Arts in 1896. He became an ordained deacon in 1894 and priest in 1895, and held a curacy in Wandsworth, after which he became preceptor of Bristol Cathedral in 1897. On 12th January 1899 he married Lillian Louisa, a daughter of Admiral Sir Richard Vesey Hamilton. He was a Minor Canon of St. George's Chapel, Windsor from 1900 to 1951. Following the death of Sir Walter Parratt, he was in charge of the choir from 1924 to 1927.

Fellowes' compassion for mid-16th to mid-17th century music led him to edit thirty six volumes of madrigals, thirty two volumes of lute songs, and twenty volumes of William Byrd's music, as well as a broad array of Tudor Church Music. His work covered not only the music, but important biographical and critical writing such as *The English Madrigal Composers,* published in 1921 and *William Byrd*, published in 1936.

Fellowes was a Fellow of St Michael's College from 1920, and honorary librarian from 1918 until 1948. It was during this time he arranged and catalogued the music library. He was followed in the post by Watkins Shaw.

Fellowes works were recognised by his *alma mater* and he was appointed an honorary fellow of Oriel in 1937, he also received honorary doctorates in music from Dublin University in 1917, Oxford University in 1939, and Cambridge University in 1950. He was interested in cricket and published *History of Winchester Cricket.* He was appointed a Member of the Royal Victorian Order in 1931 and in 1944 he became a Companion of Honour. He was President of the Musical Association from 1942 until 1947 where he helped them secure a Royal affiliation, and President of the Church Music Society from 1946 until 1951, following on from Archbishop Lang. Fellowes died at 12 Clarence Road, Clewer Within, Windsor, on 21 December 1951.

Fellowes' editions of English Tudor church music represent a very significant contribution to 20th century musical scholarship. They brought into prominence composers such as Byrd and Orlando Gibbons, whose work was thus made accessible to composers and scholars, notably Ralph Vaughan Williams, whose revision of *The English Hymnal* was influenced by study of these themes in Fellowes' editions. He lectured extensively on the subject, travelling numerous times to the United States for this purpose. His was the foremost work in the Anglican Tudor revival of the early 20th.C. His autobiography was titled *Memoirs of an Amateur Musician* (Methuen, London, 1949).

His writings apart from those mentioned above included –
English Cathedral Music (Methuen, London, 1969).
The Knights of the Garter, 1348-1939. (SPCK 1939)
Organists and Masters of the Choristers of St George's Chapel, Windsor Castle.(Historical Monographs, Vol.3) 1939
The Military Knights of Windsor, 1352-1944. (Historical Monographs, Vol. 4)
The Vicars Or Minor Canons of His Majesties Free Chapel of St George in Windsor. (Historical Monographs, Vol.5)
The Baptism, Marriage and Burial Registers of St George's Chapel, Windsor. (Historical Monographs, Vol.10)

Henry Cope Colles

Henry Cope Colles (20thApril, 1879 – 4 March 1943) was an English musician, music lexicographer, writer on music and organist. He is best known for his thirty two years as chief music critic of *The Times* (1911-1943) and for editing the 3rd and 4th editions of *Grove's Dictionary of Music and Musicians*.

Henry Colles, known informally as 'Harry', was born in Bridgenorth, Shropshire, in 1879, the son and grandson of doctors. He entered the Royal College of Music at the age of sixteen and studied music history under Hubert Parry, the organ under Walter Alcock, and counterpoint under Walford Davies. He and Davies cemented a lifelong friendship, Colles later wrote Davies' biography. He spent three years at the RCM and then, on Sir Walter Parratt's advice, applied for and won the organ scholarship at Worcester College, Oxford, graduating in 1902.

The Dean of Worcester College, William Henry Hadow, had strongly supported him to use his gift with the written word in the field of musical criticism. He became assistant music critic of The Times under J. A. Fuller – Maitland, in 1911 succeeding him as music critic. He held this position until his death thirty two years later. Frank Howes, who eventually succeeded him, said *'His writing was marked by its comprehensive taste, sure and fair judgment, and unfailing tact and humanity that tempered even his severest strictures'.*

During World War I, Colles attained the rank of Captain in the Royal Artillery and served in Macedonia, where he trained the Greek artillery in the use of British guns. For this service he was awarded a medal by the Greek government.

His arrangement of Henry Purcell's *Hornpipe in E minor* was performed at the Proms in 1915 and 1916.

In 1927, he produced the 3rd edition of Grove's *Dictionary of Music and Musicians*, which was an extensive revision of the 2nd. Edition produced by Fuller–Maitland between 1904 and 1910. In 1940 he put out the 4th Edition, a corrected reprint of the 3rd, along with a supplementary volume. He personally wrote about one twentieth of the millions of words in Grove III and IV. According to one obituarist, his assistant A. H. Fox Strangways, Colles's task was *'to put in some sort of showing, on people and things that ought to find a place there, apart from any intrinsic interest they might or might not awaken; he was, in fact, a general tidier-up of half-remembered persons and topics.'*

In 1932, Colles was appointed D.Mus. *honoris causa* by The University of Oxford. In 1934 he was appointed honorary Freeman of the Worshipful Company of Musicians. In 1936 he became an Honorary Fellow of Worcester College, Oxford.

Colles was deeply religious and he took a special interest in the Three Choirs Festival. He made an abridged edition of The Messiah for the festival. He was Chairman of the Church Music Society, Chairman of the School of English Church Music, and a Fellow and Governor of St Michael's College, Tenbury.

Henry Cope Colles died in London on 4th march, 1943, aged sixty three. When the Library of the School of English Church Music was re-opened after the war in1946, it was renamed the Colles Library in his memory.

He gave his last lecture at the Royal College of Music on March 3rd, and his last article appeared in the Times on March 5th but on the day in between, March 4th, he had gone, turning with serenity to death as one who answers the summons of a friend.

His writings apart from those mentioned above included :
Brahms (London, 1908)
The Growth of Music (Oxford, 1912-1916)
Voice and verse: A Study of English Song (London, 1928)
The Chamber Music of Brahms (London, 1933)
The Royal College of Music: a Jubilee Record, 1883-1933 (London).
On Learning Music and other Essays (London, 1940)
H. Walford Davies (London, 1942)
History of St Michael's College, Tenbury (with M. F. Alderson, London, 1943)

George Edward Pine

'George Edward Pine, who has died aged 74, was an author, poet, scholar and dedicated teacher. He was educated at St Paul's and Keble College, Oxford, where he studied classics before becoming a schoolmaster.

During the 1939–45 War he served in RAF Bomber Command as an Intelligence officer. It is said that his novel 'To Perish Never' written jointly with Henry Archer, is an excellent picture of the joys, sorrows and harrowing experiences of this part of the Service.

His scholarly works included 'The Pauline Muses', an anthology of prose and verse by Old Paulines. He edited 'The Tenbury Letters', a very scholarly collection of previously unpublished letters from eminent people discovered in the library of St Michael's College, Tenbury.

As a poet he had a delicate touch with sonnets and a charming humour in his amusing ballades. But it is in the hearts of his many former pupils whom he tutored in English that Edward Pine lives.' (Obituary, Times Literary Supplement, 1 Oct. 1983)

He taught for a time at the London Choir School which had been established before the war by Carlton Borrow (organist at SMC in 1917). He trained boys for three London churches, his own at Christchurch, Lancaster Gate, for Holy Trinity Brompton, where the Rev. Bryan Green was a very charismatic figure) and one other. During the war the London Choir School was evacuated to Kent to a fine Tudor mansion called Stonepitts Manor House near Kemsing. Every Sunday morning the boys for the three churches travelled to London and back in the evenings. Pine seems to have organised all this and made sure that the boys were always accompanied by a master. He went to St. Michael's in 1941. (He taught me Latin. The Summer Term report says I was placed 9th for Latin in a form of nine, and "*Poor*", and placed 8th for History in a form of nine, and "*Very weak*".) After he left, but I am not sure when that was, he taught at The Westminster Abbey Choir School, and it was from his time there that he wrote *'The Westminster Singers,'* published 1953. At a later date he taught at Bushey Grammar School. His *'Last Things, and Other Poems'* was printed by The Kit-Cat Press, which was a Bushey concern.

Pine retired to Ashburton, Devon, where he died. Some of these notes are contributed by The Rev. Cyril Dams, Fellow of SMC after WW ll, who was a senior cleric at The Abbey.

As the Obituary above says, he had a delicate touch with his poetry. I think the following lines give a good example of his sensitive style .

LAST THINGS

Wind has put horn to lips and blown his song
Into a tune of clouds.
Lark song is vibrant round the pillared air
To carve a frieze above the gates of dawn.

The holy sun moves from the altar'd east
And treads the pavement day: the subject airs
Bend to the winnowing and fling abroad
The frankincense of their nativity.

I like this so much, I will give some more –

TOWARD THE END OF SUMMER.

All the day long a gently-taken breath
Has drawn the perfume from the heart of things.
With subtle evanescence
Summer with her attendant swallows passed.

See where the rich blood of the year flows out,
Drains through autumnal days and, nothing loth,
Sends a transfusion to the heart of spring.

There is an unusual use of words here. For instance, Pine's use of 'tune' as a collective noun, and the sun 'treading' the pavement – it is extraordinary and I am not bright enough to try and understand what he is doing with words. In some ways he wrote in a manner which was the trend or usage of the time, and I think it would be correct to say that Christopher Fry's dazzling verbal conceits are never far away. I also sense a Tennysonian / Tithonus touch at times, particularly in *'Last Things'-'The ever silent spaces of the east / far folded mists and gleaming halls of morn, etc'.*

Pine's important connection with Henry Williamson, author of *'Taka the Otter'* must be included. There follows an extract from a very interesting letter, dated 8. 2. 1985, which Dan Symonds wrote to Tim Hollis –

'When I saw Pinny Pine in September 1980 he told me he was Williamson's literary agent and had hundreds of H. W.'s letters in the bank which he was leaving to the British Museum. They were long and interesting and worth a lot of money, and were written at the time he was writing 'Taka the Otter'. In respect for Williamson's family he was unable to publish them. Pinny first met H. W. in 1935. I asked him how it happened but he said it was too long a story; he had written it down somewhere. Pinny was "Henry's" alter ego, and H.W. wanted Pinny to live with him, but it wouldn't have worked; Williamson could not live with anyone. Besides, Pine could not afford to sacrifice his pension by giving up his teaching post at Watford. His jobs at the London Choir School, SMC and Westminster Abbey Choir School had earned him no pension at all. Pinny retired to Ashburton, Devon, where he died. He lived in a comic little house in a side street. The widow of the upstairs spare bedroom was level with the vegetable garden of the house in the next street and there was a prospect of artichokes. There was no garden, but if you craned your head over the wall of a tiny upstairs yard you could see Dartmoor, with some sheep on it. A new leather hat lay on the spare bed. We had lamb chops for lunch. Pinny spent ten minutes myopically peeling a tiny potato and then had to throw it away when he discovered it was green'.

Paul M. Griffin emailed me on September 10th 2008 as follows –
John: Good morning! I hope this finds you well.

My memory of Edward Pine is no longer very good; I was hoping to find you the obituary that was in the Daily Telegraph which I kept in my copy of The Tenbury Letters, but it has gone missing. I am certain that the Times Educational Supplement will also have had an obituary.

He started, or continued, a catalogue of the non-music part of the Ouseley Library at Tenbury. It was a privilege for a small group to help him, mainly taking books up and down the library ladders!

He read us his War Novel in draft. He told us that he had worked out the final flight in that book especially. It was not based on any of his wartime flights. I can confirm his relationship with Henry Williamson.

His biggest contribution to me personally was to start an interest in printing. At Marlborough I was master of the chapel of the Press and set and printed by hand an edition of Houseman's A Shropshire Lad, the only edition to have a preface by Houseman. This sort of encouragement was typical of Edward Pine, and I am certain there will be others who were influenced by him.

I hope these few observations are of interest and help. I would be happy to purchase a copy of your booklet in due course. All the best.'

Pine's books include –
To Perish Never - with Henry Archer (Viking Press, 1954)
The Westminster Abbey Singers (Dennis Dobson, 1953)
The Pauline Muses (Victor Gollancz, 1947)
A Bust of Ballades (The Kit Kat Press, 1981)
The Tenbury Letters - with Edmund H. Fellowes (Golden Cockerel Press, 1942)
Last Things and Other Poems (Kit Kat Press, 1962)
The Flight of Icarus and Other Poems (Arthur H. Stockwell, n.d.)

Dan Symonds

The Revd. Tim Hollis writes -

'*Dan Symonds died at Stroud shortly after his 75th birthday, and an unhappy 15 months hospitalization. He was always a puzzle to his carers!*

Dan was an only son, with two older sisters. A very private and rather eccentric person, he never married but had a wide circle of friends, largely through St. Michael's which was the real love of his life; his knowledge of its extraordinary history was unrivalled.

Dan was a pupil and chorister at the school between 1937 and 1942 (when Maxwell Menzies was choirmaster, followed by Sir Sydney Nicholson). He went on to Oundle, from where he won an organ scholarship to Hertford College, Oxford. National Service interrupted and prevented the completion of his degree; he was also wanted back at home, to work as secretary for his father's Cotswold Game Farm in Camp, near Stroud.

He was discouraged from driving a car in those days because of petrol rationing and, typically, chose to just use buses and trains for the rest of his life. Unlike his father (who must have found him hard to understand) Dan was not in the least interested by shooting parties, the functions of a village squire, or the large scale marketing of pheasant's eggs.

Unfortunately, his home belonged to the business, his freedom was quite circumscribed and he became reclusive: composing, researching, collecting, but always a lively correspondent – and once a year adventuring to the Royal School of Church Music in Croydon, where he would work for a week in the library.

St Michael's, however, remained his passion. Dan attended the annual SMC Society reunion without fail for 55 years (1947 – 2002). We sadly miss his familiar gangling figure in summer jacket and straw hat, standing on the terrace above the cricket ground, sharing his recollections and stories with us all. A gentle, witty, always interesting, companion'.

I have just spoken to my friend Tim Hollis. He told me that he conducted the service at Dan's cremation at Cheltenham Crematorium Chapel, and brought the ashes up to St Michael's at the following Commem. weekend. After the service we processed round to the east end of the church and Tim interred the ashes not far from Ouseley's grave. What more can a man do for his friend?

In his will Dan left a considerable sum to the St Michaels' Organ Fund. He also bequeathed a large amount to the Hereford Cathedral Library. It is in the Symonds Collection, Ref. D868/1 to 52.

The author too has fond memories of Dan. I particularly remember chatting away with him on the terrace on many occasions, he with his summer jacket and straw hat. Perhaps we appeared to be watching the cricket, but this was certainly not the case. We might be facing that way – we would not want to appear rude, but neither of us had any interest in sport. Our mind's eyes were focused on our endless reminiscing.

I have a letter from him dated 18th June 1998. He refers to 'Sunday' which would have been the day after our Old Boys Society Dinner. In those days we used to meet in the summer but later changed it to the Commem. weekend at the end of September, as it is now. My magnum opus which he refers to was my book on Merevale Church and the Abbey which I thought might interest him.

'D. P. Symonds, Camp, Stroud, Glos. GL6 7HJ 18.8.1998

Dear John,

I was greatly touched by your gift copy of your magnum opus and by what you wrote in it. It is good to have in tangible form a token of the many things we have in common, thanks to our shared experience at St Michael's.

Not much happened on Sunday. Only three old boys at parish mass, Beresford, Ewart and me. Afterwards Beresford and I went to see Helen Haywood-Waddington, and we saw her fabulous garden.

Then I kicked off my shoes and played the organ mousey-quietly for forty minutes before tea with the Demauses. I went in Philip Porter's open XK120 and nearly got blown away.

See you at Commem I hope. With grateful thanks, Dan'.

It is interesting that he calls it 'Parish Mass'. I would dearly have loved to have talked to him about religion, on how Anglo-Catholic was St. Michael's, and deeper matters like that, but we just seemed to reminisce all the time.

He certainly enjoyed getting a lift in an open car, and jumped at the chance of a ride down to Cadmore Lodge Hotel in my 1926 open Rolls at Reunions.

I have just read the letter to Tim, and he thought the picture of Dan kicking off his shoes and playing mousey-quietly was quite delightful.

So perhaps that is where we should leave Dan, for all eternity, playing mousey-quietly on the Father Willis.

CHAPTER FOURTEEN

CHRISTOPHER HASSALL

These two well-known personalities had strong connections with St Michael's, Hassall went there when he was ten. He was born in London in 1912, and died in 1963. His father, John Hassall, and his sister Joan, were engravers and illustrators, and his daughter Imogen was an actress. At St Michael's Hassall was appointed a Choir Monitor when he was thirteen and a half.

After leaving the College in 1925, Hassall went to Brighton College and then Wadham College, Oxford. He was a man of many talents, an actor, dramatist, lyricist and poet. His greatest fame came from his memorable fifteen year musical partnership with Ivor Novello. Hassall provided the lyrics for six long-running hits including 'Glamorous Nights' and 'The Dancing Years.' His early death, aged only fifty one, was dramatic. He died on a train at Rochester, Kent, on 25th April 1963, after suffering a heart attack whilst running for the train to see his daughter play at the Royal Opera House. Only four days earlier he had been at a St Michael's Society Luncheon in London. At The Luncheon, he had proposed the toast to The Founder, which was subsequently printed. I will print most of it here. Personally, I think it is a brilliant speech, interesting, clever and very witty. But what else would you expect from the man who wrote the librettos for Ivor Novello for fifteen years?

"THE FOUNDER"
Proposed by C. V. Hassall, Esq.

Mr Warden, gentlemen: My acquaintance with the Founder, in whose memory I have the honour to propose a toast was slight. It extended no further that to his left leg which some of you may remember, was supposed to walk the long dormitory at midnight. That was in the days when there were still partitions, two beds to a cubicle, and anything appearing unexpectedly round the corner – whether it was Thompson Two perambulating or Matron on a mission with the Gregory powder – could for a moment be strangely disquieting, and most alarming of all these apparitions was the solitary limb of Sir Frederick – six foot high, according to report. A prey to suggestion as I was (I always swallowed everything I am told) I saw so clearly, more than once, what in fact I could never have seen, that I see it still! And I'm tempted to take this opportunity of making a plea to our venerable shade: that, having got so far, he should favour us with some further portions of his anatomy, if not all at once, then a limb a year so that by 1980, or thereabouts, we may reasonably expect to find him entirely, if only obscurely reassembled. I can't imagine how that legend started. Certainly it's a most unusual one. Not even M. R. James (that Provost of King's who was such a master of the fanciful occult) ever conceived anything quite like this – a fragmentary ghost, haunting as it were, piecemeal.

Beyond this phantasmal fragment my knowledge of the Founder included the bust in the Library (see Plate 26); a good one I suspect, for I have always thought it represented someone in particular, not just a nameless local worthy who might as easily be Cicero as Arnold of Rugby. This is the face of a sensitive, scholarly, but not a forceful man. The mouth is weak, one would almost say prim. One recalls that he was a child virtuoso almost as astounding as Mozart; that he was an heir to a Baronetcy recently appointed; the heir to a social position, that is, at a time when distinctions of this kind were very sharp; that he was a child in the upper middle class growing when professional musicianship in England was not comparable with respectability, unless it was academic in character or practised in the service of the church. Certainly all the signs are that his musical gifts were prodigious, but our English Mozart grew up in a social climate altogether unfavourable, not for the poet, but for any composer who would also be a Victorian gentleman of title. I suspect that that mouth on the bust is the tell tale clue as to why the write of the superb melody "Jerusalem on High" was not a great composer, But genius will out, and, as Henry James wrote somewhere "Remarkable men find remarkable means."

Sir Frederick Ouseley, godson of the Iron Duke of Wellington, was a man of vision, and one of his, if only one, was worthy of his natural genius; and fortunately he had the financial resources to give substance to his inspiration. What resulted we now possess: a tradition that we cherish and defend, an educational was of life – as if in lieu of the collected works of an uninhibited created mind. We possess what psychologists would call the "substitute", and no one here could wish it to be otherwise. Foreigners wrote the symphonies and the operas – unless you make the exception of Arthur Sullivan. Foreigners, in the main, wrote the music, but it was an English musician who conceived the way of creating all the beauty of a Cathedral service without a Cathedral, and only in a parish church. And what a modest parish. In those it must have been small indeed, and it isn't overpopulated now! In the utmost unfrequented heart of the countryside, in the middle of a sort of bird-and-badger-haunted "nowhere" he created a "somewhere", not much on the geographer's map but a place marked in capital letters on the map of British church music.

As one thickens into plump middle age, one harks back more and more, counting the blessings. We come to realise our whole lives have been affected by Ouseley's stroke of visionary genius. With his pre-school he catches us early, when youth is wide open to whatever wind may blow, and although we may not be able to define it, we are conscious of a lasting influence. So we are grateful to him and, incidentally, our parents who had the bright idea of sending us into the sphere of his personality.

I think that through him, the Founder, we have enjoyed a peculiar advantage. We began to grow up among the values that make life worthwhile – and I don't mean our religious faith alone, which is of primary importance, nor the charm of living amongst the changing seasons of nature (though to a town-bred boy that was a marvellous discovery). No, I mean the purity of our native language in psalm, prayer and Gospel, administered in twice-daily doses, like water from a spring, and the sweet interplay of counterpoint – Literature and Music – enjoyed as part and parcel of our lives, quite independent of the world of commerce. It has always been rather easy for an Englishman to become a Philistine, but it is more difficult for an Old Boy of St. Michael's. He has less excuse.

Often I recall with pleasure that the great S. S. Wesley visited the Founder at his College. When he got back to Gloucester he wrote a short letter of thanks. One sentence in that letter puts very elegantly what many a visitor since that day, and most especially every Old Boy, will have endorsed in his heart. "Your establishment and the Clee hills," wrote Wesley, "have been subject and counter subject on which my thoughts have been playing a fugue ever since I left you." Yes, ever since you left us, Sir Frederick, your establishment and the Clee hills have been the subject and counter subject which our thoughts have been playing with pride and gratitude.

For that reason, Mr Warden, Gentlemen, let me ask you to rise while I propose a toast – The Founder, Sir Frederick Arthur Gore Ouseley.'

As I said earlier, these are great words of Hassall, and I think I concur with them all.

Sir John Betjeman did not go to St Michael's as a boy, but in later life he absolutely fell for the place. He called it *"A Tractarian dream come true"*, and enthused about it as only he could. (See his Introduction to Poem for Michaelmas Day below). Betjeman was born in 1906 in Islington where his father, Ernest, ran the family business. The company manufactured high class items such as a patented tantalus stand for cut-glass decanters, writing desks, silverware etc. Asprey's in Old Bond Street was a principle customer. Betjeman's first school was Highgate House where rather bizarrely he was taught English by T. S. Eliot (see below). He went on to the Dragon School in Oxford, then Marlborough and Magdalen College Oxford. He famously took his teddy bear, Archibald Ormsby-Gore, to Oxford with him, the memory of which later inspired his contemporary Evelyn Waugh to include Lord Sebastian Flyte's Aloysius in 'Brideshead Revisited'. John Betjeman was a poet, journalist, freelance writer, architectural commentator, broadcaster, and television personality, who was popular in England in the 1960s and 1970s and was active in the campaigning for the preservation of churches, buildings and landscape. He was knighted in 1969 and became poet laureate in 1972. He travelled extensively in Europe, North America and the Middle East between 1948 and 1975 giving lectures, slide shows and readings. He was connected with, and patron of more than 40 organizations, including Royal Commissions of Fine Art and of Historic Monuments, and The Victorian Society of which he was a Founder member. With all this public exposure, by 1962 he became Britain's most popular poet, when his "Collected Poems" sold more than 100,000 copies. He married Penelope Chetwode in 1933; they had a son Paul and a daughter Candida. In 1948 Penelope became a Roman Catholic, and the couple drifted apart. In 1951 Betjeman met Lady Elizabeth Cavendish with whom he developed an immediate and lifelong friendship. For the last decade he suffered increasingly from Parkinson's disease. In the Lent term of 1981 he made his last visit to St Michael's, accompanied by Mr. Jonathan Stedall the well-known documentary film-maker. He recalled his first visit with Christopher Hassall, and the reading of *'Poem for Michaelmas Day'*, and was determined to climb the stairs again up to the Big Dorm which brought back so many happy memories. In his letter to the Warden, Andrew Walters, he said *'You have humanized Anglican church music for me. Henry Woodyer is very pleased up in heaven and soars with the arches and calls for more spikes against the sky as some of them have fallen off. There is a magic about St Michael's which has not dimmed in any way since its foundation'*. He enclosed a generous cheque towards the fabric of the building.

Betjeman died at his home in Trebetherick in Cornwall on May 19th 1984, aged seventy seven, and is buried half a mile away in the churchyard at S$^{t.}$ Enodoc's Church. He had perhaps never been happier than as a child at Trebetherick. This is from "*Summoned By Bells*" –

> *Then before breakfast, down toward the sea,*
> *I ran alone, monarch of miles of sand,*
> *Its shining stretches satin-smooth and vein'd,*
> *I felt beneath bare feet the lug-worm casts*
> *And walked where only gulls and oyster-catchers*
> *Had stepped before me to the water's edge.*

On countless early mornings I did precisely this on Daymer Bay, during over forty family holidays in Trebetherick.

Poem For Michaelmas Day

Variations on a theme of Thomas Hood for the Centenary of St Michael's College, Tenbury.

by Christopher Hassall.

As an Introduction in the brochure for the Re-Endowment Fund in 1961, John Betjeman wrote – *'POEM FOR MICHAELAS DAY by Christopher Hassall captures the unique atmosphere of St Michael's College, Tenbury. I shall never forget my first impression of the place. There was the climb up from the little market town of Tenbury whence some of the lay clerks make their twice daily journey to Matins and Evensong to lend men's voices to the boys' choir, and there before me stretched an enormous common. In the far corner, in a land of blossoming orchards and backed by the blue distance of Clee Hill, rose a chapel, seemingly as large as Lancing. Attached to it were Warden's house, school buildings, cloister and dining hall, all in a style of the fourteenth century, re-interpreted in the style of the nineteenth century by the genius of its architect, Henry Woodyer. After Evensong, where the music was equal to the best cathedral choirs, and a walk round the building in the quiet of a Worcestershire evening, I visited the large dormitory, which runs almost the whole length of the building parallel with the chapel. Here Christopher Hassall read his poem to the boys and held them spellbound as the stars shone through the narrow Gothic windows in the gabled roof. The unique quality of St Michael's persists from the days of its Founder. The air is still charged with music. It would be impossible for any boy not to be influenced by the morning and evening thanks to his Creator which he hears so perfectly sung in this tall chapel among the orchards of Worcestershire'.*

NOTE - I have put in brackets, Hassall's eight alterations to his original version, of which I have a copy. Below the poem I have printed a letter, dated April 17th. 1956, from Hassall to Noel Kempton - Welch, concerning the structure of the poem and many other very interesting things.

I remember, I remember, grey stone, a spiral stair to bed,
The long dormitory like the creaking hold of a (Gothic) galleon,
With slit windows too high for gazing out,
Where clouds went by and the moon came searching
Through in shafts of uninvited silver;
A library, august and serious-coloured, remote as night itself,
Where the still air was tinged with sandal-wood
Mysterious with motets and Latin titles embossed
On leather bindings brown as conkers, all waiting,
Mute, compacted spine to spine, and out of reach
Of hand or understanding.

I remember, I remember, the windy cloister-walk,
The bellows, gasping and shuddering in the effort to let
Bach breath, or it might have been Widor
Demanding full-blown lungs for a dogmatic
Statement on the pedals;
St Michael painted in his triumph round the pipes,
A choir screen of wrought iron, supporting candlesticks,
A row of little ornamental dishes like top
Notes hoisted and sustained;
The English language lying open on an eagle's wings;
Music unfolding like a fair untraveled, promised land,
With meadows of flowering chords and sinuous,
(fugal) contrapuntal streams;
Merbecke, William Byrd of England, S. S. Wesley, (the word 'and'
was omitted) Walmisley (was it in D minor?) and Stanford (which was
certainly in C),
And another bird, a robin that had lost its way, flickering
Against a stained-glass patch of Galilean sky,
Unable to gain its own, contemporary, blue;
A flutter and a chirrup just audible in the (moments) timeless
Pause after the benediction.

Plate 23 The author placing a wreath near the Founder's memorial in 2012, with his daughter Kate and the Rev. Andrew Walters, the last Warden.

I remember, I remember, the tuck-shop down the road where
Marshmallow fish were three a penny;
Enormous mole-hills on the Common where for an instant
The linnets would perch and survey
The prospect as from an eminence;
Six-spot burnet moths, and the low-flying, vivid cinnabar
Whose underwing was the colour of the school magazine;
Clee Hill, away to the (left) north, huge and consoling as a psalm,
a lot of sky, and almost too many yellowhammers;
An old gypsy woman who frightened me by asking the time in
A bass voice, so deep she could have sung the
Bass part in Purcell's anthem (Jehovah quam multi)
<u>*Quae quam multi hostes*</u> *and taken the bottom E in her stride;*
An attack on a wasps' nest when we were badly outnumbered;
The thought of a letter in my pocket, the foreign stamps
She had sent me, (along) with news of my chrysalis;

Everywhere happiness, like the summer haze that hovered
Over the yellow-burning gorse and even seemed
To be spreading far, far across the border into Shropshire;
And all the while, from every aspect, wherever you were,
The grey roof of the Chapel exalted above the elm-tops,
St Michael's Chapel, reassuring, bearing witness, saying
To workers in the cider orchard, young boys
Mooching on (their) the Sunday walk, and old ones
Coming in from Tenbury for Evensong,
Saying to earth and to the heavens where the clouds from
Ludlow and Clee will forever be holding to the
Course of their serene, dissolving journeys,
Night after night whispering gravely to the radiant constellations –
God is a spirit . . . God is a spirit . . .
and we must worship him . . . must worship him . . .
in spirit and in truth.

At the beginning of this book I wrote that when we think about the place, we feel Ouseley's enduring influence on our lives in various ways, but when we picture the place in our mind's eye it is Woodyer's buildings that we see. It is not possible to think about the one without seeing the other. Hassall perfectly captures this by writing about Woodyer's *'Long dormitory like the creaking hold of a galleon, with slit windows'*, and *'wherever you were, the grey roof of the Chapel exalted above the elm-tops'*, and also about Ouseley's enduring influence by reminding us *'God is a spirit . . . God is a spirit . . . and we must worship him . . . must worship him . . . in spirit and in truth.*

Plate 24 St. Michael's College and Church, November 15th, 1862, six years after the foundation.

CHAPTER FIFTEEN

CLOSURE

It comes now to write about the College's closure. Yes, the College did close, unbelievable as it may sound, but as Robert Runcie, Archbishop of Canterbury, said in a message that Rev. Andrew Walters read out before the Service of Thanksgiving on Sunday 14th July 1985, *'The College has completed its task. But the spirit of Tenbury will live on through all those who learned to love their Church and its music at St Michael's'*. Exactly so, these are well chosen words.

It is not easy to say precisely why the College closed. In a situation like this there are many varied reasons, and I am afraid some people might have had their vested interests.

I have been told that the value of Ouseley's endowments had become almost negligible. Of course most of his money had gone on the Church and College building, and the place was under endowed from the very beginning. The school was not in debt, but with only seventy pupils, things did not look good. The Governors of Lucton School in Herefordshire, which was also struggling, were told that they would be held personally responsible if the school went into debt, and the St. Michael's Governors took fright.

I have a newspaper article of March 1985 headed RURAL CHOIR SCHOOL TO CLOSE. It is by Sarah Thompson, of the Education Staff, of possibly The Times or The Daily Telegraph. *'A rural choir school founded by a 19th century cleric and musician is to close after this summer term because of a shortage of pupils. St. Michael's College, Tenbury Wells, Worcestershire, founded by Sir Frederick Ouseley in 1845, now has fewer than 50 pupils, and needs about 80 to be viable. Mr Thomas Higginson, one of the school's trustees, said yesterday that the conditions of the supporting trust fund set up by Sir Frederick made it hard to keep open. Sir Frederick wanted the school to be an example of the finest in church music. As well as 14 choristers, the school is obliged to keep a master of music, lay clerks and a large organ in its* *chapel. Mr Higginson added: "The school is in a very isolated location, has a sparse catchment area and fewer people are sending children to private schools at ages 7-11."*

A contributory factor may have been that the church in the 1960s was looking as if it might have Catholic leanings. The Warden before Andrew Walters, Denis Paxman certainly had Popish inclinations, and when he retired he did 'cross the Rubicon', as they say. On one visit, I remember seeing the Reserved Sacrament in the Lady Chapel. A visitor reading Nicholas Pevsner's *Historic Buildings of England – Worcestershire* must have thought the same, because for a number of editions (R.C.) was printed alongside the entry for St. Michael and All Angels' Church. This indeed might have put some prospective parents off.

CHAPTER SIXTEEN

SERVICE OF THANKSGIVING

Having tried to explain why the College closed down I will now give a personal description of the Closing Service of Thanksgiving, as I experienced it.

Life had been rather difficult for me. My family business, that of manufacturing men's hats, went into a sharp decline in the 1960s and 1970s, and after nearly calling in the receiver, and of diversifying into the hosiery trade, we eventually sold the company to one of our competitor hat manufacturers. I ultimately got out of it all and retired in April 1985. It was little wonder that, on the following July 14th when I went to what was obviously a big event at St Michael's, I was unaware of what I was actually going to. I had not read my post properly. Things were obviously financially bad at the College, but I had not bothered to read the details. Perhaps I had had enough financial problems at work.

As I crossed Old Common on that sunny Sunday morning, having first checked to see the familiar chapel rooftop above the trees, I started to see a number of cars parked on both sides on the grass verge. These got more and more numerous until when I arrived at the gates of the College, it was just bedlam. There was just nowhere to park the car, and I finished up leaving it on the roadside somewhere down towards the Cadmore Brook. I walked back up the hill and in through the entrance by the west end of the church feeling somewhat numbed by the vast gathering that was there. The first think that caught my eye was a large marquee more or less filling the cloisters. The west doors of the church were open, which was unusual, and I joined a group of people walking up the wide steps. A boy approached me, and in a very polite voice – obviously a St Michael's boy – asked me if I had a ticket, and he added that the service was for ticket holders only. I mumbled something about 'Well, I am an Old Boy' and pushed on up the steps. Once inside, another St Michael's boy gave me a copy of 'SERVICE OF

THANKSGIVING', which I have with me now as I write this, and showed me to a seat – there were hardly any vacant seats left. I followed him up the north aisle and into the baptistry. He pointed me to a chair facing west not far from where Ouseley's full length portrait now hangs. The church can seat about 600.

The organ music before the service was *Sonata No. 4 in B flat – Mendelssohn (played by Christopher Robinson, Old Boy, Fellow and Organist at St George's chapel, Windsor Chapel,)* and also *Prelude and Fugue in D Major – J. S. Bach,* and *Adagio in D – Frank Bridge (played by Roy Massey, Fellow and organist at Hereford Cathedral.)* After they had both finished pounding away on the Father Willis, the service started with two longish processions. The organist for the service was Henry Rees. As the congregation stood up and started singing "Christ Is Made The Sure Foundation", the first procession started coming down the centre aisle. This consisted of representatives of The Tenbury Town Council, the Woodward Corporation, the Staff and Commoners of St. Michael's College, and the Fellows of St. Michael's College. Then the second procession consisting of The Crucifer, The Accolytes, The College Choir, The Clergy, The Archdeacon of Ludlow, The Warden, The Bishop of Hereford and the Bishop's Chaplain.

Christ is made the sure Foundation,
And the precious Corner-stone,
Who, the two walls underlying,
Bound in each, binds both in one.
Holy Sion's help for ever,
And her confidence alone.

All that dedicated City,
Dearly loved by god on high:
In exultant jubilation
Pours perpetual melody:
God the One and God the Trinal,
Singing everlastingly.

To this temple where we call thee,
Come, O Lord of hosts, today;
With thy wonted loving kindness
Hear thy people as they pray;
And thy fullest benediction
Shed within its walls for ay.

Here vouchsafe to all thy servants
What they supplicate to gain;
Here to have and hold for ever
Those good things their prayers obtain.
And hereafter in thy glory
With the blessed ones to reign.

Laud and honour to the Father;
Laud and honour to the Son;
Laud and honour to the spirit;
Ever three and ever One:
Consubstantial, co-eternal,
While unending ages run. Amen.
(Tune- Westminster Abbey by Henry Purcell,)

Obviously from where I was sitting I could not easily see everything that was happening, but it fairly quickly dawned on me what was going on. The place was closing down!

There followed the Introit hymn *Jerusalem On High,* the first of the two Ouseley hymns.

Jerusalem on high,
My song and city is,
My home when'er I die,
The centre of my bliss,
O happy place ! When shall I be,

My God, with thee, to see thy face.

The Patriarchs of old
There from their travels cease;
The Prophets their behold,
Their longed-for Prince of peace:
O happy place ! When shall I be,
My God with thee, to see thy face.

Ah me ! ah me ! that I
In Kedar's tents may stay;
No place like that on high;
Lord, thither guide my way:
O hoppy place ! when shall I be,
My God, with thee, to see thy face.

The other one, *When All Thy Mercies, O My God,* was the Offertory Hymn. (I have requested to have both of these at my funeral. Family please note. J.D.A.)

The Preparation and the Gloria followed (in Latin, I seem to remember); the service was sung to the *Missa Sancti Nicholai – Haydn.* The President was The Revd. Andrew Walters, Warden. This was followed by The Collect:

O Almighty God who has constituted the services of Angels and men in a wonderful order; mercifully grant, that as thy holy Angels do thee service in heaven, so by thy appointment they may succour and defend us on earth; through Jesus Christ our Lord. Amen.

The Old Testament Reading was taken from Ecclesiastes 44, 1-15, starting *Let us now praise famous men, and our fathers that began us.* It was read by H. G. Pitt, Esq., Fellow of Worcester College Oxford, and Chairman of the Governing Body.

The choir then sang Sir Hubert Parry's Anthem, with words from Psalm 122, *I Was Glad.*

(In 2012, many years after the College had closed, I went to a St. Michael's College Society Reunion at Michaelmas, with my daughter Kate and son-in-law, Martin. Michael Hart, who played the organ, had invited the Holgate Consort, with their lively Conductor David Barclay. Old Boys who could sing were invited to join in and Kate, Martin and I did just that, although of course I was never in the choir, and was a mere Commoner. To have the amazing experience of actually sitting in the choir stalls at St. Michael's, and singing something as exciting as *I Was Glad*, was so amazing. I was sitting on the *Decani* side, with my back against the throbbing of the mighty Father Willis, which made the occasion unbelievably special and totally memorable. As it was the year of the Diamond Jubilee, we sang the 'Vivats'.)

The New Testament Reading, 1 Corinthians 13, - *Though I speak with the tongues of men and of angels, and have not charity, I am become as sounding brass, or a tinkling symbol* was read by Patrick Smith, Captain of School.

We then sang the hymn *Praise The Lord! Ye Heavens Adore Him* – Tune: Abbot's Leigh by C. V. Taylor (Fellow).

Praise the Lord ! ye heavens, adore him;
Praise him Angels in the height;
Sun and moon, rejoice before him,
Praise him all ye stars and light;
Praise the Lord ! for he has spoken,
Worlds his mighty voice obeyed;
Laws, which never shall be broken,
For their guidance hath he made.

Praise the Lord for he is glorious;
Never shall his promise fail;
God has made his saints victorious,
Sin and death shall not prevail.
Praise the Lord of our Salvation,
Hosts on high his power proclaim;

Heaven and earth and all creation,
Laud and magnify his name.

Worship, honour, glory, blessing,
Lord, we offer to thy name;
Young and old thy praise expressing,
Join their saviour to proclaim.
As the Saints in heaven adore thee,
We would bow before thy throne.
As thy Angels serve before thee,
So on earth thy will be done.

The Gospel followed, St Matthew 18 vv 1-10, and was read by The Warden.

The Sermon was preached by The Right Reverend the Lord Bishop of Hereford, visitor to the College.

After The Creed, we came to The Thanksgiving.

Let us pray.

O God of Our Fathers, by whose grace we have come together this day to give thanks for the life and work of this College. We thank you for the abundant blessings which you have granted in the years that are past.

We remember with deep gratitude Sir Frederick Arthur Gore Ouseley, Professor of Music in the University of Oxford and Precentor of Hereford Cathedral, who by your divine inspiration founded the College of St Michael and All Angels that it might bear witness through the offering of daily worship to your unending glory.

We give thanks for all Benefactors who by their gifts enabled the Founder's vision to be fulfilled, and most especially Georgina Rushout and Montague Frederick Alderson.

We give thanks for all those who have been instrumental in spreading the Founder's ideals for the enrichment of the worship of the Church and particularly we remember Sir John Stainer and Sir Walter Parratt.

We give thanks for all those who have been called to the service of the College as Fellows, Wardens, Staff or Pupils over the past one hundred and twenty-nine years. We pray for all the present members of the College that they may continue the spirit of St Michael's in their lives.

Finally we give you thanks and praise for all those who have sustained the College, as parents, or through the work of St Michael's College Society and the Friends of St Michael's.

Finally we give you thanks and praise for the comfort and support of Saint Michael and all your Holy Angels trusting that, like them, we may reach your everlasting kingdom.

Praise God from whom all blessings flow,
Praise him, all creatures here below,
Praise him above, angelic host,
Praise Father, Son and Holy Ghost.
Amen.

There followed The Ministry of the Sacrament, The Peace, and The Offertory Hymn – Words by John Addison. Tune: Contemplation. Sir Frederick Ouseley.

When all thy mercies, O my God,
My rising soul surveys.
Transported with the view I'm lost
In wonder, love, and praise.

Unnumbered comforts to my soul
Thy tender care bestowed,
Before my infant heart conceived
From whom those blessings flowed.

When in the slippery paths of youth
With heedless steps I ran,
Thine arm unseen conveyed me safe,
And led me up to man.

Ten thousand thousand precious gifts
My daily thanks employ,
And not the least a cheerful heart
Which tastes those gifts with joy.

Through every period of my life,
Thy goodness I'll pursue,
And after death in distant worlds
The glorious theme renew.

Through all eternity to thee
A joyful song I'll raise;
For O, eternities too short
To utter all thy praise.

'Contemplation' is one of the most well-known out of all Ouseley's fifty-five hymns. Singing it as a boy, I felt particular attached to verse 3.)

The Eucharistic Prayer is followed by The Communion.

Please do not leave your seat until you are invited to do so.
The Bishop and the administrants will the carry the Sacrament to the places where it will be distributed. The Choir: At the High Altar. Those in the Nave: In front of the Screen. Those in the marquee remain seated until invited to come forward. It is hoped that on this very special occasion all those present will to receive either the Sacrament or a Blessing.
During the Communion the Choir will sing :

Agnus Dei qui tollis peccata mundi,
Misere nobis.
Dona nobis pacem.

O Lamb of who takest away the sins of the world,
Have mercy upon us.
Grant us peace.

Communion Motets.

Ave Verum Corpus – William Byrd.
Christus Factus Est – Anton Bruckner.
Bring us, O Lord God – Sir William Harris.

Let us pray.
All kneel :
President : *Father of all, we give you thanks and praise, that when we were still far off you met us in your Son, and brought us home.*
All: *Almighty God,*
We thank you for feeding us
With the body and blood of your Son, Jesus Christ.
Through him we offer you our souls and bodies
to be a living sacrifice.
Send us out
in the power of your of your Spirit to live and work to your praise and glory. Amen.

The Bishop : *May Almighty God bless the memory of the Founder of this College and all who have taught, learnt and worshiped within its walls. May God the Holy Trinity make you strong in faith and love, defend you on every side, and guide you in truth and peace; and the Blessing of God Almighty, the Father, the Son, and the Holy Spirit, be among you and among those whom you love this day and for evermore. Amen.*

HYMN

All for Jesus – all for Jesus,
This our song shall ever be;
For we have no help of Saviour,

If we have no hope in Thee.

All for Jesus – Thou wilt give us
Strength to serve thee, hour by hour;
None can move us from thy presence,
While we trust Thy love and power.

All for Jesus – at thine altar
Thou wilt give us sweet content;
There, dear Lord, we shall receive thee
In the solemn Sacrament.

All for Jesus – Thou hast loved us;
All for Jesus – Thou hast died;
All for Jesus – Thou art with us;
All for Jesus – Crucified.

All for Jesus – all for Jesus –
This the Church's song must be;
Till, at last, her sons are gathered
One in love and one in Thee.

Words: J. Sparrow Simpson
Tune: *All for Jesus*; Sir John Stainer (Organist and Fellow)

(As Stainer's strong music, the hymn *All for Jesus – All For Jesus* grew to a close, with only four, three, then two...... and then the last verse brought the hymn to its inescapable and inexorable end, it seemed to be symbolic of the College's own inescapable and inexorable closure. As the last verse was being sung it assuredly occurred to everyone that this would be the last moments they would ever again hear the St. Michael's choir sing.

Is it not felicitous that John Stainer, who was Ouseley's first organist, also wrote the last hymn? *In my beginning is my end - Eliot,* etc)

President: Go in peace to love, and serve the Lord.

All: (loudly) In the name of Christ. Amen.

THE PROCESSIONS

The Crucifer.
The Accolytes.
The College Choir.
The Clergy.
The Archdeacon of Ludlow.
The Warden,
The Bishop of Hereford.
The Bishop's Chaplain.

The Staff and Commoners,
The Fellows of St. Michael's College.
The Representatives of the Woodard Corporation,
The Representatives of the Tenbury Town Council.

Members of the Congregation are asked to remain standing until the processions have left the Church.

The Congregation then sits.

The Voluntary :Toccata (Symphony V): Widor

Later, on the lawn in front of the entrance to the College, the Warden, Andrew Walters, was saying a few words to a group of staff and handing out some cheques to Matron and some other people. In retrospect it seems very odd that he was doing it there and then, and in public, but he was and he did. It seemed to me as if the Abbot and the Prior were being paid off at the Dissolution of the Monastery, and the church, the cloisters and all the buildings would be soon as ruined and desolate as Rievaulx or Tintern. Or even Merevale.

I had had enough, and with my eyes welling up I walking back to my car and drove homewards over the Common, with tears flowing freely down my cheeks.

I felt that the greatest loss was that there would be no more boys who would have the wonderful experience that I had had of having been at St. Michael's, the experience in fact of having inherited some of Ouseley's Legacy.

I should add that today, St. Michael's College is a small international secondary boarding school offering GCSE and A Levels, University Foundation and summer courses to students from all over the world. Specialist English language provision is provided and plays a major role in the curriculum with students going on to study at universities in Britain. The church itself is still a thriving parish church, strongly supported by the local community, and well attended. A restoration fund has raised good money, and the building is now in excellent condition. This is largely thanks to Michael Hart, who is Chairman of the Restoration Fund.

Today, also, the Saint Michael's College Old Boys Society thrives. It was founded in 1905 and is very active. There is a good website (www.smcsociety.co.uk). This is a great credit to the Old Boys considering the College closed nearly thirty years ago. The current President is Guy Holland. We have over sixty members and we have a Reunion Dinner at Michaelmas after Evensong on the Saturday of the weekend.

CHAPTER SEVENTEEN

PERSONAL NOTES
Going to St. Michael's in 1941 and 2002

I suppose the journey to St Michael's starts properly when, having gone down the M5, you turn off the dual carriageway towards Ombersley and the sign includes the magic name 'Tenbury'. This was not always the route. In the early days we used to go through the centre of Birmingham, and out on the Hagley Road, then on through Kidderminster. Indeed, the very first time that I went, in January 1941, the snow was so bad that we only got as far as Kidderminster by car. Gerald and Lou (my father and mother) were determined that I should get there on my first day, at least my Mother was, and we had set off from home more or less in a snowstorm. I forget what car we had at the time, but I remember it sliding into a snowdrift on the bend near the Beehive Cottage as Gerald accelerated to try and get up the hill. By the time we had been dragged out by a tractor, which somehow appeared, the snow was even heavier, and I naturally assumed that we would abandon the idea and go home, Jack would put the kettle on, and we would have a cup of tea. However, the tractor towed us up to the top of McFarland's Hill, and from there we went on into blinding whiteness on our own, rather like Captain Scott but with a team that was not unanimous in its objectives. My Mother kept saying 'We've got to get him there today, somehow'. I was not so positive.

We slithered through the centre of Birmingham, but the snow was even worse in Kidderminster so we left the car near the station, and caught a train. At Tenbury we got on the school bus that was meeting trains, and after managing to trundle up the hill, we crossed Old Wood Common. Gerald and Lou did not look at ease, sitting with all the other small boys, my trunk and tuck box, and Mr Pine who was a new master. We eventually arrived at a building and a door with a carving of St.

Michael over it. I gave Lou a hug, said goodbye to them both, and went inside. I never did know how they got home.

However, let us get back to the present and to the Ombersley Road. It is notoriously slow as you wind around the valleys and fields, ever getting deeper into Worcestershire and Herefordshire. The great tower of Abberley beckons from the distant hilltop and eventually you are going up the hill past it, and then down into the Teme valley. After passing the Bridge Hotel, which is at last being renovated, I crossed the river and then went through Tenbury and up the winding round to Old Wood Common. In the middle of Tenbury is the Royal Oak, a timber-framed gem with a pretty Jacobean façade. This is where, during my second term, one weekend with Lou and Gerald, I had two boiled eggs for tea. Edward Pine happened to be there, with his aged mother, and told my friends. Forever after at St. Michael's I was called 'Eggy'. Before crossing the common I called at The Fountain and bought some ham and cheese sandwiches to have for lunch, whilst the cricket was on.

At the far side of the common lie the college buildings, and the first sight of the chapel roof, seen above the treetops, is a big thrill, and you really feel that you have arrived. I parked the car on the terrace overlooking the cricket field, which is, in fact, the west side of the cloisters. I think Ouseley originally planned to have buildings here, but, as with the proposed spire on the church, the money ran out. It is just as well as the three sides, made up by the church, the cloisters and the Warden's rooms, and then the college building, make a perfect unit in themselves. The open west side, with the ground falling rapidly away, makes the whole site look out to the Cadmore Brook valley and the beautiful Herefordshire countryside beyond. The layout is of course monastically correct in details as well as in general terms. The cloisters lie to the south of the church, as do all monasteries north of the Alps, or ultramontane, as we far too clever amateurs say. South of the Alps the monks needed the protection of the church for shade in the cloisters, rather than shelter from the cold north wind, and so every monastery was built the other way round, with the cloisters to the north of the church. Henry Woodyer, the architect, also correctly placed the kitchens and dining hall to the southwest, keeping the noise and the smells as far from the chancel of the church as possible. With these thoughts in my mind, I met up with Patrick Carden and my good friend Dan Symonds who all went to the school in 1939, and chatted, eating my sandwiches, whilst the cricket finished. The Society was playing The Village, and this year we won, but some of the village team looked very small boys. They were no smaller though than the society team were when they first played on this pitch. Afterwards there was tea and sandwiches in the village hall, but we went, with other friends, to the library where Jenson Jones was showing some old videos of the college and the choir. We depressed ourselves considerably by watching scenes of the closing of the college. Harry Pitt, Chairman of the Governors as well as The Fellows, explained in the video how he had no option but to shut up the shop. The trouble is, you cannot stop a ship from sinking when the first thing you notice is the water swirling about your ankles. With a realistic appraisal, years earlier, of what was happening and worldly planning, using the school's very considerable assets, Ouseley's dream need not have ended. The irony is that private education is now booming again. The fact that Ouseley's school does not exist anymore is a great sadness to us all, but the real tragedy is that young boys and girls have been denied the immensely valuable experiences and lasting influences for good that we received.

    The second video that Jenson put on was a Christmas carol service with St Michael's choir of about twenty years ago and another choir, which was recorded at Great Whitley Church. I watched it for a little while and then I started feeling restless. I don't like watching a TV screen for very long; I feel 'plugged in' like an automaton and I want to be free. I walked down the passage towards the dining hall and just wandered around for a bit looking idly at the very familiar scenes. There was no one at all about, just me and my memories. I could hardly believe that it was sixty one years when I first went there, and in a way I felt that I had never left. I happened to look at my feet and saw my sandals and shorts, which is what I wore in the summer when I was there – very odd, perhaps I hadn't left. I then went out of the front door, with the carving of St. Michael over it, and walking down the drive with my mobile, phoning the children for a chat. Emma was in, Kate was shopping (not like her) and I talked to her three children in her car, and there was no reply on Matt's. Gill was golfing.

Plate 25 The Library as it is now, with the bust of The Founder.

CHAPTER EIGHTEEN

SIR GORE'S AND SIR FREDERICK'S LIBRARIES

Before dealing with the dispersal of the two libraries, a few paragraphs would be appropriate describing the Music Library as it was when it was first catalogued by Edmund H. Fellowes. I cannot do better than quote extracts from the first three pages of Chapter XIV – *The Tenbury Music Library* – from his autobiography *Memoirs of an Amateur Musician*, Methuen, 1956. Fellowes' catalogue was printed in 1934 by the Lyre-bird Press in Paris. For the double-cubed room see Plate 26, and for the bust of Ouseley on a plinth, and surrounded by empty shelves see Plate 25.

"*One of the most important tasks that has fallen to me to undertake is that of putting in order and cataloguing the music library collected by Sir Frederick Ouseley in the nineteenth century. This collection now belongs to St. Michael's College. Ouseley's hobby was the collection of rare treatises on musical subjects, and musical books of all kinds, but especially manuscripts. His collection at St. Michael's now takes rank among the most important, not only in England, but also in Europe and America. This degree of its importance had not hitherto been realised. The gradual growth of it was due to the extraordinary flair that Ouseley seems to have possessed for discovering the existence of treasures in hidden places, as well as to his expert knowledge. He was well served by a number of discriminating buyers. Fortunately, too, he had the necessary wealth, but prices of such things were trifling in comparison with those of today. In addition to this, numbers of his friends gave him presents, chief among these being the priceless manuscript score of Handel's Messiah which the composer used when conducting the first performance of that famous work in Dublin in 1742.*

It was at the funeral of Sir Hubert Parry in St Paul's Cathedral in the autumn of 1918 that I happened to meet William Barclay Squire. He asked me whether I would undertake the much-needed task of putting Ouseley's music library into order.

We now come to the immensely sad fate of the two libraries after the closure of the College in 1985. What precisely happened to all the music manuscripts and printed books is a rather complicated story, but it is sufficient here to say that most of the music went to the Bodleian Library, as bequeathed in the Founder's Will, and most of the printed Oriental books were bought by Grant and Shaw Ltd, of Edinburgh.

The Bodleian website writes it up as follows - Collection Level Description: <u>Music Manuscripts from the Library of St Michael's College, Tenbury, Worcestershire</u>. Reference: MSS Tenbury 296-304, 308-848, 851-1386, 1442-471, 1473-93, 1495-513, 1515. Title: <u>Music Manuscripts from the Library of St Michael's College, Tenbury, Worcestershire</u>. Dates of Creation: [c. 1600]-1930. Extent: 1156 shelf marks.

Extract from the Bodleian Website

The manuscript collection of St. Michael's College, Tenbury was almost entirely the achievement of one man, the founder of St. Michael's, the Rev. Professor Sir Frederick Gore Ouseley, Bart. Ouseley was himself a major figure in Victorian music, as composer, bibliophile, scholar, and practical musician. He was Professor of Music at Oxford from 1855 until his death in 1889, and founded St. Michael's College in 1854 as a collegiate society maintaining a regular chapel choir, in the hope that the standards of church music would be improved and restored following the decline which musicians such as S. S. Wesley had done much to identify. The collection of manuscripts which Ouseley managed to acquire, and which he placed in the library, reflects not only his own musical taste, but also the continuing interest which English musicians showed for the music of previous generations, particularly church music, a notable feature also of Dean Aldrich's library at Christ Church, Oxford, which dates from the beginning of the previous century. In each case the later musicians were interested to transcribe and study the earlier music, though it does seem that the habit, common

Plate 26 The Library as it was originally.

in Aldrich's time, of arranging and adapting music had become much less noticeable by the time of Ouseley. Certainly these collectors served their generation (and ours) very well by preserving large numbers of manuscripts. The collection is in three main parts: English music of the 16th, 17th, and 18th centuries, especially church music; Continental music (mainly Italian) of (mainly) the 18th century; and music of Ouseley's own time, including much by him. There are some extremely important manuscripts in the first group, notably the Batten organ-book (MS 791), several sets of part-books made in England by Catholic recusants in the late Tudor and early Stuart periods (e. g. MSS 341-344, 354-358, 389 for predominantly English music, some of it from the mid-16th century, and MSS 349-353, 359-363, 369-373, 374-378 and 379-384 for Continental motets, though music by Byrd seems to have been a sine qua non in such anthologies) and also some secular music of the same period (e.g. MSS 364-368, 940-944, 1016, 1019). Ouseley's original collection was supplemented by the discriminating skill of E.H. Fellowes who added MSS 1464, 1469-1471 and 1486. English music of the 17th and 18th centuries included important sources of instrumental music (MSS 296-299, 390, 302) and church music (e.g. MSS 310, 620, 621, 651, 680, 702, 737, 787, 789, 797-803 etc), including some reputable Handel sources in the hand of his amanuensis J.C. Smith (e.g. Messiah, MSS 346-347), and several Chandos Anthems, MSS 614-617 and 881-883, and other works MSS 884, 885), and Blow's Coronation Anthems (MS 1008), Purcell's Dido and Aeneas (MS 1266) and Arne's Judith (MS 985). Manuscripts of particular note in the Italian group include a large number of Paisiello operas, and also operas, oratorios, and church music by many of the leading Italian composers of the 18th century including Alessandro Scarlatti, J.C. Bach, Hasse, Cimarosa, Pergolesi, Marcello, Perez, and Jommelli. The presence of such works in this collection (as in other collections ranging from Aldrich's, mentioned above, to those of later collectors now housed in the British Library or the Royal College of Music), is a clear indication of the continuing influence of Italian music and the ubiquity of manuscripts from the Italian manuscript-copying-houses.

Music of the Victorian period is represented by a large collection of Ouseley's own works, and of his transcriptions of earlier music, a task undertaken partly out of sheer interest, but partly as an aid to the preparation of the lectures which he gave as Professor at Oxford. There are also important sources for Crotch (his oratorios The Captivity of Judah and Palestine) and various others such as Vincent Novello, S.S. Wesley, Stainer, Prout, and Sterndale Bennett.

The Tenbury collection includes autograph material by Arnold, Boyce, Blow, Croft, Cooke, Burney, P. Hayes, Simpson, Travers, and S. Wesley, and Purcell, in addition to autograph annotations by Handel in the copy of Messiah. Amongst the Continental manuscripts are autographs by Pachelbel, Dumont, Galuppi, Contumacci, Pergolesi and Colonna, and several sources copied by Abbe Santini. In the 19th century group we find autographs by Bishop, Spofforth, Prout, Pratt, Stainer, Jebb, and of course Ouseley himself.

The most famous single item in the entire library was Handel's conducting manuscript of the The Messiah (Tenbury MSS 346 – 347), the first performance of which was at a charitable concert in Dublin on Monday the 12th April 1742.

The score began its existence as a neat copy for Handel's personal use by his man-of-affairs and amanuensis, John Christopher Smith. Handel finished composing *Messiah* on 14 September 1841, and this copy was ready for him to take to Ireland in November, and to be used in Dublin on April 12th.

Later History of the Messiah Conducting Score

After Handel's death the manuscript passed to John Christopher Smith, his friend and secretary, and then to Smith's son who had been the composer's pupil. Afterwards it passed through other hands until it came to William Young Ottley (1771-1836). Ottley's library was sold in 1838 when the score was knocked down for one guinea, which would be about £40 in today's money. Ottley's nephew Captain E. J. Ottley (an original Fellow of St Michael's) then managed to acquire it, and he presented it to Ouseley in 1867. Since then it has become known as the

'Dublin' score, or the 'Ouseley' score. It is now known as 'Tenbury MSS 346-7.

The dilapidated condition of both volumes necessitated their rebinding in 1920, when the leather of the original covers were pasted down on the inside of the new ones. In the 1940s a small fire-proof room was built in what was called the railway room, with a door leading into the Library. The score was kept here in two oblong cardboard boxes, one containing Part I and the other Parts II and III. Prior to this the two boxes were on the open shelves in the Library. They are now housed in specially lined boxes, together with rest of Ouseley's music library in conditions of the greatest possible safety, at the Bodleian, thanks to generous donations made for the purpose by the Pilgrim Trust and by Miss Hascall of New York.

There has been a serious misunderstanding about what was or what was not scribbled by Handel at the top of various pages in the score. There is the fairly well-known story that when he arrived in Dublin for the concert he found that the local divas had been vying with each other as to who was going to sing the solos. This applied to *'There were shepherds'*, *'How beautiful are thy feet'* and *'I know that my Redeemer liveth'*. The story goes on that Handel was adamant that he preferred the voice of a boy treble. In the event he chose the soloist he wanted, and to make sure of it he wrote *'The Boy'* at the head of *'There were shepherds'*, *'How beautiful are thy feet'* and *'I know that my redeemer liveth'*. The words *'The Boy'* are written in thick red pencil. Sir Sydney Nicholson writes up this story fully, and fictionalised, in his *'Peter, The Adventures of a Chorister, 1137 – 1937'*. Sir Sydney writes -

'The copy he used still exists, and if you were to go to Tenbury you would see it in the library of St Michael's College, and you would still find those words written, first faintly in black and then clearly in red the words 'The Boy'.

I am sorry to have to say this, but I am afraid Sir Sydney is wrong. I have had the page photographed by the Bodleian. In fact, the title page of *'I know that my Redeemer liveth'* has "The Boy" in pencil, not in red crayon, but more importantly, it is crossed out. The name of the soloist, written in red on this page is *"Sigra. Frasi"*. 'Sigra.' is the abbreviation of Signora. Another name scribbled in red in this manuscript is 'Masson'. This is Handel's spelling of the soprano Mason, and it is particularly interesting because she only sang for Handel once, and that was in Dublin. This proves that this manuscript was used for the first and Dublin performance in 1842.

By chance I happened recently to buy a copy of *Messiah* with eight autographs including Michael Tippett, whose copy it probably was, Isobel Baillie (twice), Gladys Ripley, Walter Widdop, Norman Walker, Doreen Hunter, and Malcolm Sargent (twice).

In 1946 Sir Malcolm Sargent made a recording of *'The Messiah'* for Columbia Records with the Huddersfield Choral Society and the London Philharmonic Orchestra. This score is connected to the soloists and musicians who produced that record.

I turned to page 167 to see if there was a name of the soloist who sang *'I know that my Redeemer liveth'*. There, boldly written, was the firm autograph of Isobel Baillie. It was like a message from beyond the grave, from Handel himself, saying 'No, I've told you before, this does <u>not</u> have to be sung by The Boy'.

Michael Tippett had a particular association with *Messiah*, namely that he took from it its tripartite formal design which was to become the overall outline of *A Child of Our Time*. Tippett describes this association.

'The shape of Messiah is tripartite. The first part is all prophecy and preparation. The second part is epic from the birth of Christ to the second coming, judgement, millennium and world's end. The third part is meditative: chiefly, the words of St Paul. Incomplete performances grievously impair this wonderful shape. But I have always observed and admired it. I decided to accept this format for A Child of Our Time, keeping a first part entirely general, restricting the epic material to a second part, and using a third part for consequential comment'.

The more specific nature of Tippett's own version of the tripartite scheme is outlined by him in the following description of the overall design.

'This three part division works out for A Child of Our Time in the following way. Part I deals with the general state of oppression in our time. Part II presents the particular story of a young man's attempt to seek justice by violence and the dramatic consequences; while Part III shows the moral to be drawn, if any'.

The first London performance of the Messiah, when King George II famously stood up, took place at Covent Garden Opera House on March 23, 1743.

The Crouch Fine Arts Library

Baylor Libraries, Baylor University, Waco, Texas, U.S.A. Baylor Libraries is part of Baylor University, a Baptist foundation and the first university to be established in Texas. It was founded in 1845. Their website contains the following - *'The Sir Frederick Arthur Gore Ouseley Collection'.* Purchased in June of 1991, the Ouseley Collection contains 297 books and scores from the library of Sir Frederick Arthur Gore Ouseley (1825-1889) and includes hymnals, anthems, cathedral books, organ music, part songs, madrigals, oratorios, and operas as well as books on music history, singing, organ construction, bell ringing, acoustics, and music theory. Rev. Ouseley was an English church musician, scholar, and composer who established St Michael's College, Tenbury in 1854. He was an outspoken proponent of fine church music. As a result of his efforts as a church musician, the parish church at St Michael's became well known for its excellent service music. Ouseley was also a noted collector of music.'

APPENDIX ONE

THE ORGAN

by

Michael Hart, G.R.S.M., A.R.C.O.

One of the cornerstones for Ouseley's plans for St. Michael's was to have the church Offices sung twice daily to a high standard. For this a good organ was essential and he commissioned Messrs Flight and Son to build a 4 manual organ, the specification of which he designed himself. There was no organ case as such. The front pipes were all polychromed by George Frederick Bodley, the upright ones being painted with figures and mottoes relating to the dedication of the church. The Tuba Mirabilis pipes projected outwards "En chamade".

"En chamade" (French: "to sound a parley") refers to powerfully voiced reed stops in a pipe organ that have been mounted horizontally, rather than vertically, in the front of the organ case, projecting out over the choir stalls. They produce a commanding, loud trumpet-like tone, used for fanfares and solos. Any stop mounted en chamade will be much louder than a stop elsewhere in the organ, even though in church organs the stops stand on the same wind pressure.

The Tuba Mirabilis was put to good use as follows. On Commemoration Day, Saturday 3 October 1863, the seventh anniversary of the foundation was celebrated. There was evensong on the eve of Michaelmas Day. As the local newspaper reported *'The anthem for showing off the powers of the magnificent organ, especially the Tuba Mirabilis, was "Sleepers Awake" by*

Mendelssohn'. When the chorale *'Sleepers Awake'* is performed nowadays, it is not unusual to perform it unaccompanied except for a brass section. When you hear a recording, you hear the choir singing the first perhaps 8 bar phrase and the brass bashes in. You can well imagine what the Tuba Mirabilis mounted 'En Chamade' would have sounded like in the wonderful acoustics at St Michael's.

The Specification of the 1856 Flight Organ.

Great Organ, 14 Stops, CCC to g3 in altissimo, 5 2/3 octaves

1. (Stop Diap.Treb.	metal)	8ft. tone
(Stop Diap.Bass	wood)	
2. Clarabella Treble	wood	8ft.
3. Small Open Diap.	metal	8ft.
4. Large Front Open Diap.	metal	8ft.
5. Stopt Flute	wood	4ft. tone
6. Gamba Principal	metal	4ft.
7. Large Principal	metal	4ft.
8. Twelfth	metal	22ft.
9. Fifteenth	metal	2ft
10. Tierce	metal	1 3/5ft
11. Full Mixture	III ranks	1ft
12. Sharp Mixture	III ranks	2ft
13. Trumpet	reed	8ft
14. Tuba Mirabilis	reed	8ft

All the stops in the Great Organ are carried down to the CCC key, except the Clarabella, the Flute, and the small Trumpet.

Choir Organ, 11 Stops, CCC to g3 in altissimo, 5 2/3 octaves

15. Stopt Diapason	wood	8ft. tone

16. Dulciana	metal	8ft.
17. Viol da Gamba	metal	8ft.
18. Flute, stopt, metal to Tenor c. bass wood		4ft. tone
19. Principal	metal	4ft.
20. Twelfth	metal	2ft.
21. Fifteenth	metal	2ft.
22. Flageolet	wood	2ft.
23. Sesquialters	III ranks	1 3/5ft.

All the stops in the Choir Organ are carried down to the CCC key, except the Dulciana, Viol da Gamba, and Flageolet, which only extend to CC, and the Flute and Cromorne, which end at Tenor c.

Swell Organ, 10 Stops, CC to g3, 4 2/3 octaves

26. Bourdon	stopt wood	16ft. tone
27. Stopt Diapason	metal	8ft. tone
28. Open Diapason	metal	8ft.
29. Principal	metal	4ft.
30. Fifteenth	metal	2ft.
31. Mixture	V ranks	2ft.
32. Double Trumpet	reed	16ft.
33. Trumpet	reed	8ft.
34. Hautboy	reed	8ft.
35. Clarion	reed	4ft.

Solo Organ, 9 Stops, Tenor c to g3, 3 2/3 octaves

36. Double Stopt Diap	wood	16ft. tone
37. Stopt Diapason	wood	8ft. tone
38. Keraulophon	metal	8ft.
39. Harmonic Diapason	metal	8ft. tone

40. Wald Flute	wood	4ft.
41. Piccolo	wood	2ft.
42. Mounted Cornet. V ranks to middle c1 only		
	wood & meta	18ft.
43. Vox Humans	reed, metal	8ft.
44. Spare Slider for a reed stop		

Pedal Organ, 4 Stops, CCC to Tenor f, 2 1/2 octaves

45. Pyramidon, down to GG key		32ft. tone
46. Open Diapason	wood	16ft.
47. Quint	wood	10ft.
48. Principal	wood	8ft.

Couplers

1. Swell to Great.
2. Choir suboctave to Great.
3. Swell to Choir.
4. Swell 8ft pitch to Pedal.
5. Choir 16ft. pitch to Pedal.
6. Great 16ft. pitch to Pedal.

The church was duly consecrated on the Feast of St Michael and All Angels, the 29th September 1856. Sir Frederick organised a large choir including the boys from Lovehill House and representatives from Hereford and Worcester Cathedrals. There were also some boys from the Chapel Royal including a young Arthur Sullivan who sang a solo. Dr George Elvey, organist of St George's Chapel, Windsor Castle, played the organ.

In 1866 the Flight organ suffered from a leaking roof where water had penetrated the sound boards and ruined the many working parts of the organ. Probably the leaking roof was not noticed until the organ showed signs of not working properly by which time irreparable damage had been done. Obviously there had to be a complete rebuild. Sir Frederick had wanted to ask Flight to carry out the work but Dr Stainer who had been organist at St Michael's 1857–9 aged 16 advised Sir Frederick to approach an up and coming young organ builder from Rochdale called Thomas Harrison. This turned out to be a great mistake, one which Sir Frederick bitterly regretted. The sorry saga which followed is both long and tedious. We have in the church records 81 pages (each 12 inches by 6 inches) written in long hand probably by the college solicitors Norris and Miles recording all the correspondence between Sir Frederick and Harrison the organ builder.

It starts with Harrison sending Sir Frederick the specification for the new organ dated 19th December 1866:

The organ to consist of 4 manuals CC to G 56 notes and pedal organ CCC to F 30 notes.

GREAT ORGAN

1. Double Open Diapason	metal 16ft	56 notes
2. Double Stopped Diapason	wood 16ft	56 notes
3. Open Diapason	metal 8ft	56 notes
4. Stopped Diapason	wood 8ft	56 notes
5. Clarabella	wood	8ft 44 notes
6. Flute		8ft 44 notes
7. Principal		8ft 56 notes
8. Gamba Principal		8ft 56 notes
9. Twelfth		56 notes
10. Fifteenth		56 notes
11. Tierce		56 notes
12. Mixture	3 Ranks	168 pipes
13. Mixture	2 Ranks	112 pipes
14. Trumpet		56 notes
15. Clarion (all new)		56 notes
16. Small Open Diapason	8ft	56 notes

SWELL ORGAN
Of 10 stops not to be altered

CHOIR ORGAN
1. Spitz Flute (all new)	8ft	56 notes
2. Dulciana	8ft	56 notes
3. Stopped Diapason	8ft	56 notes
4. Rohr Flute	4ft	44 notes
5. Principal	4ft	56 notes
6. Twelfth	3ft	56 notes
7. Fifteenth	2ft	56 notes
8. Flageolet	2ft	56 notes
9. Cremona (lower 12)	8ft	56 notes
10. Sesquialtra	3 ranks	168 pipes
12. Voix Celeste (New Rank)	8ft	44 notes

SOLO ORGAN
1. Spare Slide (Double)		
2. Spare Slide (Cornet)		
3. Stopped Diapason		56 notes
4. Keramlophon		44 notes
5. Harmonique Clarabella		44 notes
6. Wald Flute (12 new)		56 notes
7. Harmonique Flute (12 new)		56 notes
8. Piccoio (12 new)		56 notes
9. Vox Humana		56 notes
10. Tuba Mirabilis		56 notes

PEDAL ORGAN
1. Double Open Diapason	Wood	32ft 30 notes
2. Open Diapason	Wood	16ft 30 notes
3. Open Diapason	Metal	16ft 30 notes

4. Open Quint	Wood	12ft 30 notes
5. Bourdon	Wood	16ft 30 notes
6. Open Flute	Wood	8ft 30 notes
7. Principal	Metal	8ft 30 notes
8. Twelfth	Metal	6ft 30 notes
9. Fifteenth	Metal	4ft 30 notes
10. Tierce	Metal	3ft 30 notes
11. Mixture	5 Ranks	150 pipes
12. Bombarde (18 new pipes)	Metal and Wood	16ft 30 notes
13. Trumpet	Metal	8ft 30 notes
14. Violone	Metal (prepared for)	16ft 30 notes

COUPLERS
1. Gt to Ped
2. Sw to Ped
3. Ch to Ped
4. Solo to Ped
5. Ch to Gt
6. Sw to Gt
7. Solo to Gt
8. Sw to Ch
9. Six double action composition pedals
10. Two double action composition pedals added

The total cost would be £286-10s.

On February 1867 Sir Frederick gave Harrison the go-ahead to start rebuilding the organ. The next letter from Sir Frederick to Harrison is dated September 1868. Twenty months have elapsed since Harrison was told to start work and Sir Frederick is complaining about the slow work and lack of progress in rebuilding the organ particularly as the annual commemoration was once more at hand. He says that had Harrison sent the pipes and other materials required and extra men, the organ would have been finished in time. Sir Frederick gives Harrison two options:

1. Send men, pipes and materials and get the organ finished.
2. Let what there is of the organ already in situ be put in order and made serviceable, and then let an arbitrator be called in to appraise the work already done by Harrison and balance it against the money already paid by Sir Frederick, and then the whole affair can be wound up and taken out of Harrison's hands. Sir Frederick finishes by saying he will not consult his lawyer until he receives a reply from Harrison.

On September 8th Harrison replies saying he has been ill for many weeks and unable to attend to his business: he had also met with an accident after recovering from his illness which afflicted him for a further 2 months.

Many letters were written by both Sir Frederick and Harrison through December 1868 and January 1869. Harrison proposes that he finishes the organ in time for Easter Day 1869 but quibbles about the costs with Sir Frederick not willing to pay more. The costs have gone up to £677 in March 1869. In June 1869 Harrison's wife writes to say that her husband has been ill again for the past month and has gone away to re-couperate at the seaside.

Correspondence continues with Harrison pleading for more money and Sir Frederick steadily losing his patience over the whole affair. There were times when Harrison's workmen went off to pick fruit in the local orchards because they had no work to do as pipes and materials had not been sent. I quote a typical letter from Harrison to Sir Frederick dated 8th July 1869:

Sir,

Absolute necessity is the only plea under which I can ask you again to help me. I must raise a certain sum of money by Saturday next and I beg you to let me have £180. The I O U which I enclose for that sum leaves all existing contracts, clauses etc. entire and you can pay me the I O U at the finish in cash.

Your obliged and obedient Servant
T H Harrison

On August 30th 1869 Sir Frederick writes a very strong letter to Harrison as follows:

Dear Sir,

I have recently come home and am very much disappointed at the state in which I found my organ. Considering that I have advanced you more money than you could claim from me and have given you every facility for getting the whole thing done, I may fairly complain. Matters are now come to such a situation that I must come to some final arrangement with you. If you are unable to finish the organ (as I am disposed to think you are) I must at once call in someone else for I must and I will have my church prepared for my approaching anniversary festival. I should rather have half the organ really playable than it be in the horrible state it is now in. The pedal touch is so stiff that it is next to impossible to play the pedals. The bellows action is a complete failure. The keys rattle and are very unpleasant and loose. In short I am thoroughly disgusted and out of all patience. I ought to have allowed the original builder to rebuild the instrument and I regret now that Dr Stainer advised me otherwise. I have been also put to very great inconvenience to raise money to pay you for what after all you have not as yet done what (I begin to think) you never will. And which makes me more angry you appear to take no interest in the work although you told me it was "to make your reputation"!! Then again I must complain that after all there will be no room for your much vaunted piston action so that you cannot carry out your own agreement although I have paid such a large sum in advance. Altogether I think I am justified in saying that you have treated me shamefully and everyone thinks so too. Of course you have lost my good word which you might have secured and you ought surely to have known your own interest better. The least you can do now is to come here at once in person and patch up at least some of the organ and clear out of my church. I have spoken to a great many persons and they all take the view of the matter only they use rather stronger language than I care to employ in writing to you. I know indeed that you will say you have been a loser too by the job, that that is no compensation to me and i may fairly retort that if so you ought not originally to have undertaken such a work as this.
I shall send a copy of this letter to Dr Stainer who has enquired after the progress of the organ and of course I shall keep a copy myself. Hoping to see you here at once if possible.

> *I am Dear Sir*
> *Yrs faithfully*
> *FAGO*

Harrison continues to write that he cannot complete the work without further payments. Dr Stainer has said he will inspect the organ when Sir Frederick says the work is finished. He is not prepared to do this and lists all the many faults on the organ which must be put right first. In a letter dated January 11th 1870 Sir Frederick refuses Harrison's request for a further payment of £100 until the organ is certified as completed. On January 17th Harrison again asks for more money as he has to pay an amount by the following Saturday. Finally on February Sir Frederick's solicitor, William Norris writes the following letter to Harrison:

Sir,

Sir Frederick Ouseley has handed me your letter to him applying to him for further remittances on A/C of his organ and has instructed me to inform you that he declines to make any such remittance for two very sufficient reasons. First: that you have not fulfilled your contract, the organ being still in a very incomplete and unsatisfactory state and secondly, because he finds he has already paid you more than you would be entitled to if the work had been completed. I am further directed by Sir Frederick to request that all further communications be addressed to me.

> *Yrs faithfully*
> *Wm. Norris*

There follows 5 pages of accounts which add up to nearly £1,300. Harrison then sends a telegram to Norris demanding £200 otherwise his solicitors will proceed without further notice.

Feb 19th 1870 - Norris proposes to refer the whole matter to the arbitration of Mr Kettle of Wolverhampton, the County Court Judge and Trades Referee with Mr Nicholson of Worcester (or some other Organ Builder to be mutually agreed upon) as assessor.

Feb 20th 1870 - Harrison replies and offers to complete the large bellows and other small matters at his own cost and guarantee the organ for 2 years if Sir Frederick pays him £200. Then he should be paid a further £175 and give Harrison a satisfactory Testimonial.

Same date - Harrison writes again to Morris saying that as the matter cannot be settled amicably, he would prefer taking it to the assizes. He blames the problems on Sir Frederick for demanding many extra things being done.

Feb 24th 1870 - Harrison writes to Norris to say he has discussed the whole situation with his solicitors and having weighed the matter in its various points and considering Sir Frederick's position in the musical world and the length of time which must elapse before the question can be heard, he has decided to offer to accept 300 guineas and a satisfactory Testimonial in full discharge of his claims if paid by Saturday next the 26th.

Feb 25th 1870 - Norris replies that having discussed his proposals with Sir Frederick, he declines to pay one farthing more than £200 in full discharge of his account.

There is now a break in correspondence until Harrison writes to Sir Frederick on October 29th. Even though the court case is still pending, Harrison is arguing that his poor financial situation is due entirely to his building the St Michael's organ.

Harrison writes again to Norris again On May 4th 1871 asking if there is a desire to come to an amicable settlement of the matter.

On May 8th Norris replies first that the organ is now in a disgraceful state as to materials and workmanship. The only proposal Sir Frederick has is:

To refer the whole matter to any of the following London organ builders: Mr Walker, Messrs Gray and Davison, Mr Holditch or Mr Bryceson, but only upon the following conditions: that the arbitrator shall be at liberty to award to Sir Frederick such amounts as he shall find to be over paid. Also such amounts as he shall find due for breach of contract and costs that previously to such references your assignees shall enter into a personal bond for payments to Sir Frederick of such amounts as the arbitrator shall find due to him.

On May 13th Harrison writes to Norris to say that he cannot possibly accept the terms of his proposal.

A new figure now appears on the scene. A year has passed since the last letter from Harrison. On 22nd May 1872 Norris receives a letter from

Thomas Horridge of Glossop. He informs Norris that he has purchased the organ factory and business from Harrison to free him from his Inspectors and to give him another start in life. Harrison was obviously bankrupt. Horridge suggests that he and Norris meet so the matter could be settled amicably without proceeding to law.

On 27th May Norris replies that after the treatment Sir Frederick has received at Harrison's hands, he declines to enter into any communication with him until the proceedings now going on are brought to a close.

On 29th May Horridge replies that in Harrison's ledger there is a balance owing of £296-2-3 which his solicitor says is clearly due. He suggests they meet to discuss the matter fairly and accept a sum to be agreed upon in settlement of the A/C.

On 30th May Norris replies that Sir Frederick declines to pay one farthing in settlement of his claim. He also says that he is quite at liberty to come and inspect the organ.

On 1st June Horridge writes to say that he will come over to Tenbury the following Monday with WT Best of Liverpool (a well known organist of the time). Also coming will be Mr Hill of London and Mr Jardine of Manchester.

On 4th June Horridge says he has decided to write this final letter without prejudice. There cannot be 2 opinions about the workmanship of the organ. It is very good and the materials are the best. He has talked the matter over with Mr Best and he accuses Sir Frederick of preventing Harrison finishing the work. He offers Sir Frederick three propositions:

1. Complete the organ as it now stands.
2. Rebuild the organ and place Pedal Stops where large bellows are now.
3. Build a new organ entirely.

He will have either of the schemes fully carried out in 12 weeks from the agreement being signed. He will take the organ over to Rochdale and bring it back finished. His terms are:- £250 down payment and 5 further bills when the organ is completed.

On June 8th Sir Frederick replies that he is unable to accept any of Horridge's proposals. It is evident that his opinion of the character of the mechanism of his organ differs too radically from his own to admit further discussion.

On June 11th Horridge replies that he will withdraw the action now pending, if Sir Frederick can show him a good and sufficient reason why he should do so. He says the organ is valued at no less than £4000 and Harrison has charged about £1200. He feels the matter ought not to go to court. Horridge admits that Harrison has caused Sir Frederick great annoyance and begs him to suggest a way of settling the matter to avoid either party spending needless money.

On June 15th Sir Frederick replies to Horridge that he should withdraw the action as he has already paid more than he ought and in this view he is supported by the recorded opinions of Messrs Telford of Dublin, Nicholson and Willis (organ builders) as well as Dr Monk, organist of York Minster and of Mr Walker Joy of Leeds - not to mention many others. They have all pronounced the work bad, the materials defective and the charges exorbitant. Sir Frederick goes on to say that if he thinks the organ is worth £4000, he is willing to let him have it (with the exception of the painted pipes) for £2000 if all law proceedings be quashed finally at the same time.

Horridge replies on June 19th saying that when he mentioned the figure of £4000, he meant that that was the figure any London organ builder would have charged him. He makes a further offer to Sir Frederick without prejudice. The disputed balance is £296: half of that is £148. Say £100 and I will send you a receipt in full discharge when he receives the cheque. If he does not agree to this, the trial must proceed.

On June 21st Sir Frederick replies that he will not pay one farthing more.

There follows 24 pages which concern the case going to law. The first 9 pages describe in detail the history of the case.

Then a 3 page witness statement by Sir Frederick.

Then a 4 page witness statement by the St Michael's organist, Langdon Colborne.

Then a 1 page witness statement by Dr Stainer.

Then a 3 page witness statement by John Nicholson of Worcester.

Then a 2 page witness statement by William Telford of Dublin.

Then a 2 page witness statement by Dr Edwin Monk, organist of York Minster.

We have no record concerning the outcome of this case. As Harrison had been declared bankrupt, it is more than likely that neither party went to law, but this is purely guesswork.

The Father Willis Organ

We have the actual "Articles of Agreement" drawn up on 21st April 1873 between Henry Willis and Sir Frederick Ouseley. Willis promises that he will dismantle the organ, transport it to his London Organ Works. He will use only the best parts of the organ and make those pipes he uses speak like Willis pipes. He will return it to St Michael's, erect it and have it in good working order within a period of 5 months. The referees will be William Ellis of Monkstown, Dublin and Edward Hopkins, organist of the Temple Church, London. If the organ is not ready in time, Willis agrees to pay Sir Frederick £5 per week. The cost of the organ will be £1000 and Sir Frederick agrees to pay the transport costs from St Michael's to Willis' organ works in London and back.

Specification of the Organ

Pedal Organ

1. Contra Bourdon	wood	32ft.
2. Open Diapason	wood	16ft.
3. Open Diapason	metal	16ft.
4. Violone	metal	16ft.
5. Bourdon	wood	16ft.
6. Quint	wood	10 2/3ft.
7. Octave	wood	8ft.
8. Violone Cello	metal	8ft.
9. Super Octave	metal	4ft.
10. Fourniture		5 ranks
11. Bombard		16ft.
12. Clarion		8ft.

Choir Organ

1. Viola da Gamba	metal	8ft.
2. Dulciana	metal	8ft.
3. Lieblick Gedact	wood	8ft.
4. Caribel Flute	wood	8ft.
5. Lieblich Flote	wood	4ft.
6. Gemshorn	metal	4ft.
7. Flute harmonique	metal	4ft.
8. Piccolo	wood	2ft.
9. Corno de Bassetto		8ft.

Great Organ

1. Bourdon	wood	16ft
2. Double Diapason	metal	16ft
3. Open Diapason	metal	8ft
4. Open Diapason	metal	8ft
5. Stopped Diapason	metal & wood	8ft
6. Claribel Flute	wood	8ft
7. Principal	metal	4ft
8. Flute harmonique	metal	4ft
9. Twelfth	metal	3ft
10. Fifteenth	metal	2ft
11. Fourniture		3 ranks
12. Mixture		2 ranks
13. Tromba		8ft
14. Clarion		4ft

Swell Organ

1. Bourdon	wood	16ft
2. Open Diapason	metal	8ft
3. Salicional	metal	8ft
4. Voix Celeste	metal	8ft
5. Lieblich Gedact	metal & wood	8ft
6. Principal	metal	4ft
7. Fifteenth	metal	2ft
8. Mixture		5 ranks
9. Contra Fagotto		16ft
10. Cornopean		8ft
11. H. Hautboy		8ft
12. Clarion		4ft
13. Vox humana		8ft

Solo Organ

1. Gamba	metal	8ft	(Gift of Mr Ellis)
2. Flute harmonique	metal	8ft	
3. Concert Flute harmonic	metal	4ft	
4. Como di Bassetto	metal	8ft	
5. Orchestral oboe & bassoon		8ft	
6. Tuba		8ft	

Couplers

Solo to Gt

Solo to Ped

Sw to Gt

5w to Ped

Ch to Gt

Gt to Ped

Sw to Gt Sub oct

Ch to Prd

Sw to Gt Sup oct

SW to Ch

3 Pedal Nentrils to Gt

3 Pedal Nentrils to Sw

3 Pedal Nentrils to Ped

The Keys and Pedals will be new.

The blowing apparatus to be so arranged as to be easily worked by 2 men.

Willis was as good as his word and the organ was returned to St Michael's, erected and in good working order to the satisfaction of the 2 referees within the specified 5 months.

In 1895 the solo organ was enclosed in a box including the Tuba which is not normally enclosed. The solo box virtually touches the vaulting and in spite of the distance from the console, the pipes speak clearly and respond well.

In 1916 some major work was done to the organ under the direction of Dr George Sinclair, organist of Hereford Cathedral. He was an Old Boy of the college and had been a pupil there when Willis rebuilt the organ. He was also a close friend of Sir Edward Elgar (Enigma Variation X1 GRS). The action of the organ was originally 'Barker Lever' and in 1895 the pedal organ was fitted with pneumatic action. Now similar action was fitted to the rest of the organ with a new console. The organ was cleaned and overhauled throughout. Mains electricity did not reach the college until 1950. In 1919 the college had installed a dynamo which ran on paraffin to supply electricity to the college and the church. Sadly Dr Sinclair died in 1917 and it was decided to install an electric blower to provide wind for the organ in memory of Dr Sinclair. There is a plaque on the wall, east of the organ screen recording this event. No longer would 2 men be required to pump the organ. It was installed by Taylor of Leicester. There was just one problem - as soon as the organ blower was turned on, all the lights in the college and church dimmed!

In August 1951, Henry Willis and Sons wrote a report on the organ. It was found to be extremely dirty (there would have been 35 years' worth of dirt and bird droppings). Some of the pipes and reeds had been seriously damaged due to unauthorized entry by some of the boys. The pneumatic action was found to be in perfect order. All the pipe work is on 3 inch wind and only the Great and pedal reeds and the solo tuba are on heavy pressure. The pitch of the organ was a quarter tone sharp. At this time the Revd. Noel Kemp-Welch was warden (Headmaster of the college and vicar of the parish) which was fortunate as he was a musician. He had been a chorister at St Michael's and a choral scholar at King's College Cambridge under Boris Ord. It very much concerned him that young musicians at St Michael's were going into the outside world with the wrong sense of what was perfect pitch. The college centenary was looming (1956) and Mr Kemp-Welch felt rightly that important cleaning and restoration work should be carried out so that the organ would be in perfect working order in time for the centenary. It was decided the following work should be undertaken:

1. A complete overhaul, clean and restoration, lowering the pitch and re-voicing the solo Gamba.
2. Completion of prepared accessories (solo and choir pistons).
3. Conversion of swell pedals to the balanced type.
4. Replacing swell Vox humana with Lieblich flute 4ft.
5. Replace Great Flute harmonique 4ft by Principal No 2.
6. Swell Contra fagotto and solo orchestral oboe to be returned to the factory for repair and re-voicing.

Willis guaranteed that the whole operation of lowering the pitch would be carried out in a manner ensuring the retention of the original tone colours and giving a complete and artistic result. It was also decided to move the organ blower from the outer vestry into a separate blower house outside the church to eliminate the noise it made. The total cost for all this work was going to be £2583-19-6d. The contract was signed and it was agreed that work would start after Easter 1953. The south aisle was roped off and turned into a workshop and storage area for the many hundreds of pipes. The daily offices in term time were still sung regularly using the piano when necessary. No scaffolding was used, just tall ladders: there were no 'health and safety rules' then. The organ builders were billeted in the village.

The organ was ready for use at the beginning of the Michaelmas term. The author (Michael Hart) was asked by Kenneth Beard, the organist and Master of the choristers to play the hymn after an evening Litany. As was his wont he liked to make a big noise and for the last verse of the hymn used full organ. On releasing the final chord there was a tremendous crashing sound which was particularly frightening to a 12 year old. I immediately turned the blower off. The warden and Mr Beard came rushing into the organ chamber to see what had happened! The bellows have weights on them to give extra wind pressure. The weights on the smaller of the 2 bellows at the front of the organ had been incorrectly placed. After the last chord was played there was a rush of wind which tipped the top of the bellow up resulting in the weights crashing to the ground breaking through the pedal trackers. Willis obviously did the necessary work to repair them and to replace the bellow weights correctly free of charge. When it came to paying the last instalment of Willis' bill, it was found that the parish was £760 short. A generous parishioner lent the money interest free and it took another 2 and a half years to clear the debt. In 1918, when the college installed its own generating plant, electric lights were installed in both the college and church. Also an electric blower was placed in the outer vestry so that no longer were the services of two men needed to pump the organ.

In 1975 when Harrison & Harrison were maintaining the organ, a humidifier was installed to combat the drying effects of heating and so prolong the life of the leather and wood in the instrument. The pedal board was found to be one note out to the right. If you were expecting to play C your foot was in fact on a B. For obvious reasons pedal boards today are uniform and a fault like this would have caused problems to visiting organists and indeed to the resident organist if he was going to play an organ elsewhere. So a new pedal board was installed.

Other alterations included removing 2 stops entirely - the Great Quint 5 1/3ft and the violincello from the solo. On the choir, the 2nd flute was removed as was the 2nd 4ft flute which was placed on the great in the space left by the Quint. The viola da Gamba was moved to the solo organ to replace the violincello. To fill the 3 vacant ranks on the choir, three new stops were installed: a Nazard 2 2/ 3ft, a Tierce 1 3/5ft and a 3 rank mixture.

The college sadly closed in 1985 and the organ became the responsibility of the parish. It would have been easy for them to consider getting rid of the Father Willis organ as after all an electric machine with no maintenance costs would be more than adequate to accompany the hymns during the one weekly service now held in the church on a Sunday. But the PCC with strong and wise leadership have taken their responsibilities seriously, appreciating the importance of St Michael's in the History of English Church Music. The organ is very much part of our heritage and the parish has raised the necessary money to maintain this wonderful instrument. In 1990 the heavy pressure reservoir was re-leathered together with other re-leathering work at a total cost of £8,821.

In 2010 it was realised that the leather of many of the sound board power motors could no longer be patched and needed re-leathering together with the 4 upper anti-concussion bellows. Also it had been a long time since the interior of the organ had been cleaned. Two firms were approached for estimates and we accepted that of Nicholson of Malvern, a highly respected local firm who had looked after the organ in the past. The total cost was £36,300 plus VAT at 20%. We already had some money in the organ fund, but a great deal more was needed. The parish, with only just over 80 on the electoral roll was very supportive. One group called "Down Memory Lane" donated all their profits which was a 4 figure sum. Dr Christopher Robinson, a college Old Boy and formally organist of Worcester Cathedral, St George's Chapel, Windsor Castle and St John's College, Cambridge, ran a very successful choral workshop in church with all profits helping to swell the organ fund. He also gave us the name of a Trust which supported financially the restoration of historic organs, and it gave us £12,000. The College Old Boys donated over £7,000 and various small amounts from funerals and weddings all helped. Nicholsons were given the go-ahead and started dismantling the organ at the beginning of October 2011. This time a scaffolding tower had to be built over the Decani choir stalls going right up to the vaulting so the painted pipes could be removed and access gained to the rest of the organ. As planned the work was completed in time for the carol service in December. Many people commented how much brighter the organ sounded as a result of the smaller pipe-work being cleaned. Nicholsons had done a splendid job and we were well satisfied.

The following black and white photographs of the interior of the church were taken before 1919 as that was the year electricity reached the church and there are still oil lamps in situ.

Specification Of The Organ In The Church Of St. Michael And All Angels, Tenbury Wells

Great

Bourdon	16
Double diapason	16
Open diapason I	8
Open diapason II	8
Stopped diapason	8
Claribel flute	8
Flauto traverso	4
Principal i	4
Principal ii (1953)	4
Twelfth	2 2/3
Fifteenth	2
Fourniture	3 ranks
Mixture	2 ranks
Tromba	8
Clarion	4

Pedal

Contra Bourdon	32
Open wood	18
Open metal	16

Violone	16
Bourdon	16
Quint	10 2/3
Violincello	8
Principal	8
Fifteenth	4
Mixture	5 ranks
Ophicleide	16
Clarion	8

Swell

Bourdon	16
Open diapason	8
Lieblich Gedact	8
Salicional	8
Voix celeste	8
Lieblich flute (1953)	4
Geigen principal	4
Flageolet	2
Mixture	5 ranks
Contra fagotto	16
Hautboy	
Cornopean	8
Clarion	4

Choir

Lieblich Gedact	8
Dulciana	8
Lieblich flute	4
Gemshorn	4
Nazard (1975)	2 2/3
Piccolo	2
Tierce (1975)	1 3/5

Mixture (1976)	3 ranks
Corno di bassetto	8

Solo

Viola da gamba	8
Flute harmonique	8
Concert flute	4
Orchestral oboe	8
Clarinet	8
Tuba	8

APPENDIX TWO

THE BELLS

by Chris Pickford

The Ecclesiastical District of Old Wood was created in 1856 from parts of the parishes of Tenbury Wells, Leysters, Bockleton and Middleton on the Hill, with the newly erected church of St Michael & All Angels as its parish church. The church was built in 1854-6 to the designs of Henry Woodyer and consecrated on 29 September 1856. With the adjacent College, it was largely funded by Sir Frederick Arthur Gore Ouseley who used his family wealth to establish a choir school to promote and develop the traditions of Anglican church music. The College founded by Ouseley closed in 1985 and the buildings are now used by an international college. The church remains in parochial use and the choral tradition is maintained by visiting choirs.

The church is a tall cruciform building with an apsidal chancel, transepts and an aisled nave. It is linked by a cloister to the College buildings on the south. Woodyer originally intended that the church should have a western cloister and a south west tower, but this was never built. The two small bells are accommodated in recessed openings above the great window in the west wall of the church, and the clock movement is housed in the roof space over the crossing. Access to the clock and bells is by a steep iron ladder in the north transept and thence by walkways over the timber vaulted ceilings of the church.

The apertures for the bells were carefully designed for the purpose. The stonework is moulded with a curved inner surface where the bells swing, and there are sliding doors behind the bells to prevent cold air and debris from getting into the roof space. There are slots in the stonework below the bell-wheels for the ropes, which were drawn on pulleys to fall to one side of the area at the west end of the church. The bells are as follows:

Bell Inscription

1	WARNER & SONS LONDON 1856
Waist:	(*Royal Arms*) PATENT
2	WARNER & SONS CRESCENT FOUNDRY LONDON 1855
Waist:	(*Royal Arms*) PATENT

The physical data

Bell	Founder & date	Dia	Note	Nom	Moulding	Cwt Qrs Lbs
1.	John Warner & Sons 1856	19⅜"	A+43	1805	2:2 - 2:3:2	1. 3. 0.
2.	John Warner & Sons 1855	21⅛"	Ab+6	1667	2:2 - 2:3:2	2. 1. 0.

The bells are the originals, supplied when the church was built in 1854-6. They were cast by John Warner & Sons of the Crescent Foundry in London. They bear the Royal Arms and Patent on the waist, and they have angular canons. They were both originally hung to swing with wooden stocks, strap gudgeons, stock hoops, wall-mounted bearings, traditional wooden bell-wheels and clappers. The smaller bell was hung in this manner with its original fittings and swung until its rehanging in 2008. The larger bell had its wheel removed in 1922 when the clock was installed, a steel plate having been fixed above the stock to prevent it from being swung. From that time it was used only for the clock.

During repairs to the main roof in 2007-8 both bells were lowered to the ground for rehanging. The work was carried out by Arthur C. (Bill) Berry of Malvern, the cost being met from the bequest of Dan Symonds. The bells were rededicated at evensong on 27 September 2008. The smaller bell is now hung for swing chiming with a wooden stock, strap gudgeons, stock hoops, ball bearings and iron chiming lever. It is fitted with a new clapper suspended from an independent staple and it has been turned so the clapper strikes on the less worn soundbow on the opposite side of the bell. The larger bell is still fixed, but an internal trigger-action clapper has been fitted so that it can be chimed for services.

History

Of the existing bells there is no more to add, but the brief ownership of two bells – offered to the church but never hung – is worth recording here. These bells are mentioned in the main published histories of the College, although these sources differ on points of detail. Thanks to information that has recently come to light in the records of John Taylor & Co, the Loughborough bellfounders, with confirmatory material from the Croydon foundry archives, it has been possible to put together a full account of the affair which, until recently, had been a slightly mysterious reference in the College history.

The PCC minutes indicate that the bells were offered to the church by Captain Paul Butler in 1923. The offer was accepted, and the bells arrived in the following year. Butler was one of the original choristers at St Michael's in 1856-7 and later a Fellow of the College until his death, aged 82, in 1926. Taylors' records provide the following details of the bells:

Bell Inscription

1	GILETT & JOHNSON 1900
2	GILETT & JOHNSON 1900

Waist:	THESE TWO BELLS AN OFFERING FROM PAUL J.H. BUTLER 1900

In addition, the following words were painted on the waist of each bell

PER SS. GALEKA VERY REV^D. THE DEAN S^T SAVIOUR'S CATHEDRAL PIETERMAURITZBURG NATAL

The physical data

Bell	Founder date	Diameter	Note	Cwt. Qrs. Lbs.
1.	Gillett & Johnston 1900	35¾	B flat (956 Hz)	8. 2. 6
2.	Gillett & Johnston 1900	41	A flat (818 Hz)	12. 0. 12

The records of the Croydon bell foundry show that these bells were cast by Gillett & Johnston in September 1900 for St Saviour's, Pietermauritzburg, in South Africa. In the books they appear as numbers 1742 (a 35½" bell weighing 8-3-0) and 1743 (a 41" bell of 12-1-0). Given the date, it would seem that the Boer War prevented these bells from reaching their intended destination. Butler evidently took possession of them himself, and eventually – almost a quarter of a century later – made arrangements for the College to have them.

The lack of a belfry made it an impractical gift, and in their 1943 history of the College Alderson and Colles noted that "it was found impossible to hang them". Instead, it was decided to sell them and to apply the proceeds on the erection of two carved oak organ screens, one for the front of the organ in the chancel, and one for the side in the south aisle. These were put up as "a memorial to Captain Paul Butler and purchased with money realised by the sale of two bells which had been his gift". The bells were sold to John Taylor & Co in December 1927 through Hewitt, the Tenbury builder. The clock was installed in 1922 as a memorial to the second Warden of the College, the Rev. John Hampton, who died in 1922. The erection of the clock is recorded on a brass plate near the pulpit inscribed:

> TO THE GLORY OF GOD
> AND IN THE MEMORY OF THE
> REV JOHN HAMPTON, MA
> WARDEN OF THIS COLLEGE
> AND VICAR OF THIS PARISH
> 1889 – 1916
> THE CLOCK WAS PLACED IN THIS CHURCH
> MICHAELMAS 1992

The clock is a two-train movement signed on the setting dial by "J.B. Joyce / Whitchurch". It has a cast iron flatbed frame, a going train with pinwheel escapement and a striking train. It shows the time on cast iron skeleton dials beneath the gable-ends of the two transepts and strikes the hours on the larger bell. It was hand-wound until 2008 when it was converted to auto-wind with funds from the Dan Symonds bequest.

There is also a small call bell (not examined) in the gabled turret on the west front of the main College buildings.

Visited: CJP 18 June 2006 and 7 October 2008 (after rehanging); Thanks to Michael Hart and Bill Berry.

APPENDIX THREE

BIOGRAPHICAL DETAILS OF PLATE TWENTY SEVEN

I am grateful to Charles Beresford for these biographical notes.

1.1 William Claxton. He was a boy at St Michael's from 1862 to 1868. The choir's repertory for 1865 includes a service by him in E flat. He was subsequently organist there from 1877 to 1886 and taught Canon Alderson. In 1883 a school concert included a March that he had composed for the Band of those in the choir. *(Shaw p.42)* The 1885 choir repertory includes two anthems and a service by him in G *(Shaw p.122)*. The latter was performed at Michaelmas 1899 *(Bland p.134)*.In 1883 Ouseley wrote to Alderson's father expressing concern that Claxton had been 1883 Ouseley wrote to Alderson's father expressing concern that Claxton had been negligent in his music lessons teaching Alderson. He was a violinist and leader of the orchestra at Tenbury Music Society's concert on 1st July 1885 when Ouseley's Oratorio *the Martyrdom of St Polycarp* was performed *(Bland p.80)*. He also composed some madrigals performed at concerts of this society. He was a violinist and leader of the orchestra. Claxton was ordained in 1887 and was Vicar of Navestock from 1897 to 1921. He was a Fellow of St. Michael's from 1894 until he resigned in 1921. He died in 1933.

1.2 Marmaduke Morris. Rev. Marmaduke Charles Frederick Morris of York (1844-1914) Composed some madrigals performed at concerts of the Tenbury Music Society. Claxton was ordained in 1887 and

Plate 27 The Tenbury Music Society Orchestra in 1866.

was Vicar of Navestock from 1897 to 1921. He was a Fellow of St. Michael's from 1894 until he resigned in 1921. He died in 1933.

1.3 C. Helmore. Rev. Frederick Helmore of Canterbury was a clarinettist and had known Ouseley at Oxford. His brother Rev. Thomas Helmore (1811-1890) had founded St Mark's College, Chelsea, and trained the choir at St. Barnabas Pimlico when Ouseley was there around 1850. *(Bland pp 43-44).* He was also Master of the Choristers at the Chapel Royal from 1846 and one of the Priests in Ordinary from 1847 *(Grove).* He sent his son to St Michael's, "in spite of his enthusiasm for, and Ouseley's dislike of, plainsong".*(Shaw p.40).* Perhaps this C. Helmore was that son?

1.4 Sale. A long shot, but Grove includes a George Charles Sale (1796-1869) who was a chorister at St Paul's under his father John Sale. George was organist of St George's, Hanover Square, from 1826. *(Grove)*

In the Band list there was also a Mr B Sale of Shrewsbury, who was a violinist.

1.5 Colbourne. Dr Langdon Colborne of Hereford (1837- 89) was a violinist. He had succeeded Stainer as organist at St. Michael's in 1859. His service in D and two anthems were in the repertoire in both 1865 and 1885. His services in B flat and C, and a third anthem, were also in the 1885 repertoire. *(Shaw pp.122, 125)* He left after 14 years and, was organist at Beverley Minster, Wigan and Dorking then was appointed organist of Hereford Cathedral in 1877.*(Shaw p.132)* He conducted Ouseley's *"Martyrdom of St Polycarp"* at the Three Choirs Festival there in 1888.

1.6 Dunscombe. Rev Duncombe of Hereford was a bassoonist

1.7 Hawksmore

1.8 Mann. Richard Mann (1837-69) was a Lay Clerk from 1857-64 and his anthem *Grant we beseech thee* was in the repertoire in 1885 but not in 1865 *(Shaw p.127).* In 1866 he published *A Manual for Singing,* about the training of choristers, which was revised by John Stainer ten years later.

He should not be confused with Dr Arthur Mann (1850-1929) who directed the music at King's College, Cambridge, from 1876 and composed several significant pieces.*(Grove)*

1.9 Bartholomew. Mr R Bartholomew of Ludlow played the viola.

2. These others were not on the list of those *augmenting* the Tenbury Music Society, so they may have been local members.

2.1 Charles Corfe. **Dr** Charles William Corfe (1814-1883) was appointed organist of Christ Church Cathedral Oxford in 1846,after Ouseley as an undergraduate had covered the duties in the interregnum following Dr William Marshall's resignation. *(Bland p.36)*. Corfe conducted the chorus in the first performance of *The Martyrdom of St Polycarp* that Ouseley submitted for his degree of Doctor of Music in 1854 *(Bland p.58)* He was among the singers at the consecration service of St Michael's in 1856. *(Shaw p.32)* His anthem *Thou Visitest the Earth* was in the choir repertoire in 1865 *(Shaw p.125)*.In the same year he and Ouseley approved Stainer's oratorio *Gideon* for Stainer's Mus. Doc., and the three of them subsequently worked alongside on the examination of Oxford Music degrees among other musical activities.*(Dibble p.109)* Corfe's sons were two of the first boys at the newly established St Michael's. *(Bland p.106)*. Dr Charles John Corfe (1843-1921) was an assistant master at St Michael's 1864-7, then a Chaplain RN and became a Fellow in 1888. He was Bishop of Korea 1889-1905. An oil painting of him by an unknown artist hung in the Dining Hall. His brother Canon Edward Charles Corfe (died 1937) was at St Michael's 1863-8 and became a Fellow in 1884. *(Shaw p.118)* In 1916-7 he acted as Warden in the interregnum after Revd. Ryley's resignation from ill-health and the appointment of Revd. Swann, *(Shaw p.49)*.

2.2 CF Fox-Chawner. 1840-67. He was an "Adult Commoner" from 1863-7, with 3 anthems listed – 1 in 1865, 1 in both 1865 and 1885, and 1 in 1885. *(Shaw p.125)*. His ordination and early death at the age of 27 indicates that the photo was taken not later than 1867.

2.3 Fred Davenport

2.4 Frank Davenport. Francis William Davenport (1847-1925) was a fee-paying boarder rather than a chorister at St Michael's. *(Shaw p 41)*. He went on to be a professor at the Royal Academy of Music from 1879 and at the Guildhall School of Music from 1882. He was also a composer and author *(Grove)*. If the photo pre-dates 1867 he would have been under 20. Does this match the photo?

2.5 Barnes
2.6 Donkin
2.7 Barratt
2.8 Blyth
2.9 Barlow Simpson

REFERENCES

Dibble, J. 2007 John Stainer : A Life in Music.
Bland, D. 2000 Ouseley and His Angels.
Watkins Shaw (ed.) 1986 Sir Frederick Ouseley and St Michael's Tenbury
Colles HC (ed.) 1940 Grove's Dictionary of Music and Musicians (4th edition.)

SOURCES CONSULTED AND BIBLIOGRAPHY

Alderson, M. F. and Colles, H. C. – *History of St Michael's College, Tenbury,* S. P. C. K., 1943.

Benson, J. Allenson – *The Messiah. History of the Oratorio,* Wm. Reeves, n.d.

Bennett, Frederick – *The Story of W. J. E. Bennett: Founder of St Barnabas, Pimlico, and Vicar of Froome-Selwood,* Longmans Green, 1909.

Beresford, Charles (Ed.) – *Memories of St Michael's, Tenbury.* 2006.

Bland, David – *Ouseley and his Angels,* David Bland, 2000.

Clark, Kenneth – *The Gothic revival,* John Murray, 1988.

Fellowes, Edmund H., C.H. – *Memoirs of an Amateur Musician,* Methuen, 1946.

Fellowes, Edmund H., C. H. and Edward Pine (Editors) – *The Tenbury Letters,* The Golden Cockerel Press, 1944.

Gatens, William J., - *Victorian Cathedral Music in Theory and Practice,* C.U.P., 1986.

Joyce, F. W., M.A. – *The Life of Sir F. A. G. Ouseley, Bart.,* Methuen, 1896.

Havergal, Rev. Francis T., D.D. – *Memorials of Frederick Arthur Gore Ouseley, Bt, M.A.,* Ellis and Elvey, 1889.

Henderson, John and Jarvis, Trevor – *Sydney Nicholson and his 'Musings of a Musician',* R.S.C.M., 2013.

Hughes, Kristine, - *Everyday Life in Regency and Victorian England, From 1811-1901,* Writers Digest Books, 1998.

Lewis, Michael J. – *The Gothic Revival,* Thames and Hudson, 2002.

Nicholson, Sydney – *Peter, The Adventures of a Chorister,* Capella Archive, 1944.

Ouseley, Revd. Sir Frederick A. G., - *The Position of Organs in Churches*, The Musical Association, 1886.

Proceedings of The Musical Association, 16th Session, 1889-1890, Novello, Ewer, 1890.

Ollard, S.L. – *A Short History of the Oxford Movement*, A. R. Mowbray.

Wainwright, David – *Broadwood By Appointment*, Quiller Press 1982.

Walsh, Walter – *The Secret History of the Oxford Movement*, Church Association, 1899.

Watkins Shaw – *Handel's Conducting Score of Messiah*, O.U.P., 1962.

Watkins Shaw (Ed.) – *Sir Frederick Ouseley and St Michael's, Tenbury. A Chapter in the History of English Church Music and Ecclesiology.* Published for The Trustees of St. Michael's College, Tenbury by the University of Birmingham. 1988.

White, James F. – *The Cambridge Movement*, Wibf and Stock, n.d.

O God, who has brought us near to an innumerable company of angels,
and to the spirits of just men made perfect:
grant us during our earthly pilgrimage to abide in their
fellowship, and in Your heavenly country to
become partakers of their joy;
through Jesus Christ our Lord and Saviour.
Amen.